COLONIAL REVIVAL *MAINE*

COLONIAL REVIVAL *MAINE*

Kevin D. Murphy

With a preface by Earle G. Shettleworth, Jr.

and contributions by
Kim Lovejoy
Rosalind Magnuson
Roger G. Reed
Earle G. Shettleworth, Jr.

PRINCETON ARCHITECTURAL PRESS

OLD ENTRANCE — KENNEBUNK

For Sandy

Contents

Earle G. Shettleworth, Jr. at Mount Vernon
in 1954

Arland Dirlam, Shettleworth House, 1940–41, Portland

Preface

IN HIS 1969 BOOK *American Architecture and Urbanism*, Vincent Scully wrote, "By the time of the Philadelphia Centennial of 1876, the country was decisively embarked on a colonial revival which has, in one sense, never entirely subsided." Indeed, the colonial revival has been a powerful force in shaping American taste down to the present day, and colonial revival architecture has been a defining element of Maine's seacoast, as this book demonstrates. Two manifestations of the movement played a major part in shaping my passion for architecture and historic preservation—my parents' house and their encouragement of my interest in history through travel.

After their marriage in 1935, Earle and Esther Shettleworth began planning for the eventual construction of a house in Portland, Maine. The children of immigrant fathers, my parents sought assimilation into the American middle class through their careers in business and teaching, which continued unscathed throughout the Great Depression. A long vacation in 1938 took them to Washington, D.C. and Virginia, where they toured the White House, the Custis-Lee Mansion, Mount Vernon, and Williamsburg.

With these icons of classical design in mind, the Shettleworths started their search for an architect in the late 1930s. Locally, John Calvin Stevens's firm was known to them through my mother's friendship with Rebecca Stevens, the wife of John Calvin II. However, my parents were attracted to the work of a young Boston architect, Arland Dirlam, after visiting a house he designed in Belmont, Massachusetts, which had been built by one of my father's business associates. The crisp symmetry, inviting Georgian doorway, and handsome brick ends of the Van Fleet House conformed to my parents' vision of the suburban ideal, and in 1940 they commissioned Dirlam to design a similar home for them at Hersey and Clifton streets in a developing neighborhood overlooking Back Cove and the Portland Peninsula.

Completed on the eve of World War II for approximately $16,000, 126 Hersey Street featured a gracious blend of traditional elements: a broken-scroll pedimented doorway flanked by a pair of bay windows, a central staircase with a balustered handrail, and a spacious living room with a large neoclassical fireplace. More contemporary in nature were the cyprus-paneled library, the basement recreation room, the screened sun porch, and the automatic garage door. Dirlam's attention to custom-designed architectural detail, coupled with the quality of prewar construction, made the house a pleasing and comfortable environment in which to raise two children, my sister and me, in the 1940s and 1950s.

Growing up in colonial revival surroundings nurtured my early interest in American history. Once my parents recognized my fascination for the past, they encouraged it through reading, collecting, and travel. The Portland of my youth suffered from a serious architectural inferiority complex, in that the city had been destroyed four times between 1676 and 1866, resulting in a Victorian brick environment that was frowned upon in the 1950s. To see real colonial buildings meant taking wonderful family trips to Portsmouth, Newburyport, Salem, Marblehead, Boston, Sturbridge Village, Newport, and Mystic Seaport, as well as to my father's maternal ancestral towns of Guilford and Madison, in Connecticut. The vacation itinerary also extended beyond New England to Philadelphia, Alexandria, Mount Vernon, and Williamsburg. These family trips to America's historic places created lasting memories. One of my earliest is visiting Mount Vernon and being told by a guard to remove my cap in George Washington's parlor out of respect for the father of my country.

Looking back from a perspective of more than forty years, I realize what sources of strength my parents' home and their support of my quest for the past were. National concerns about the arms race, the Suez Canal, and the Cuban missile crisis have given way to anxieties about the Middle East and bio-terrorism. Despite immense pressures from all sides for change, however, New England's tree-lined streets with their parade of white houses staunchly remain. In Scully's words, "Civilized withdrawal from a brutalized society encouraged interminable summer vacations to Nantucket, Martha's Vineyard, and the coasts of Massachusetts and Maine, where the old houses weathered silver, floating like dreams of forever in the cool fogs off the sea." These buildings continue to define, as much as rockbound shores, the special character of Maine's seacoast that has made it a refuge for more than a century.

EARLE G. SHETTLEWORTH, JR.

Acknowledgments

THE GENESIS OF this project goes back twenty years to an exhibition on the work of William E. Barry, which was mounted by Sandra S. Armentrout and Joyce Butler, who were director and curator, respectively, at the Brick Store Museum. Their work provided the basis for the master's thesis on Barry that I wrote in 1985, under the direction of professors Richard Candee and Keith Morgan at Boston University. Each of these individuals has continued to support my research on Barry and his contemporaries in various ways over the course of the past two decades, and I am deeply appreciative of their efforts.

The immediate impulse to revisit my work on Barry and to expand it into a book came from discussions with my colleague at the City University of New York Graduate Center (CUNY) Professor William Gerdts. Marcene J. Molinaro enthusiastically supported an exhibition on colonial revival architecture in the Kennebunks at the Brick Store Museum, which opened in April of 2002. In the course of preparing both the exhibition and this book, I was greatly assisted by Earle G. Shettleworth, Jr. of the Maine Historic Preservation Commission; Lorna Condon of the Society for the Preservation of New England Antiquities; Katherine Vaillancourt, former curator of the Brick Store Museum; Tom Johnson, curator of the Old York Historical Society; and my research assistant, Susan A. Nowicki. Martin J. Perschler of the Library of Congress contributed many references to the bibliography, and Carol Lees, of the CUNY Graduate Center, provided assistance with the illustrations. Additionally, I was fortunate that many leading scholars of Maine and colonial revival architecture agreed to contribute to this volume, and that J. David Bohl was able to photograph many of the buildings herein discussed. Nancy Eklund Later, a brilliant former student and now editor at Princeton Architectural Press, made many useful suggestions as to how the manuscript could be improved, as did Nicola Bednarek, also of Princeton Architectural Press; any remaining faults or omissions are my own. The owners of homes and other buildings designed by the architects discussed here graciously provided access to their properties. Finally, Mary Anne and Lilla Haley Caton granted me many evening and weekend hours away from them; I hope that this book is adequate compensation and a fitting tribute to our shared passion for things Maine. ❧

KEVIN D. MURPHY

Kevin D. Murphy

THE COLONIAL REVIVAL AND
MAINE, AN INTRODUCTION

Kitchen of McIntire Garrison, York, circa 1700–10, as appointed and photographed in 1936

Like to a plank of driftwood, tossed on the watery main,
Another plank encounters, touches, parts again;
Thus tossing, drifting ever on life's unresting sea
Men meet, and greet, and sever, parting eternally.

CONTEMPLATING THE SURVIVAL of some fragments of the famed John Hancock House of 1737 in Boston, demolished amid protest in the mid-1860s,[1] Madelene Y. Wynne was inspired to quote these lines from ancient Sanscrit. Published in *The House Beautiful* in 1900, the sentiments of this popular writer echoed those of many at the turn of the century. Wynne was impressed by "this drifting apart of things from things, of man from man; ever conscious of an irresistible undercurrent in the tide of life—time and chance."[2] Granted that the sensation that time worked to separate people and their tangible manifestations—"things"—was perhaps universal, the historical phenomenon of modernization in the nineteenth century only intensified the feeling. As the Western world grew more urban and industrialized, many people began to believe that premodern ways of life—and especially their physical remnants, historic buildings—were more apt than ever to be lost to the process of change.

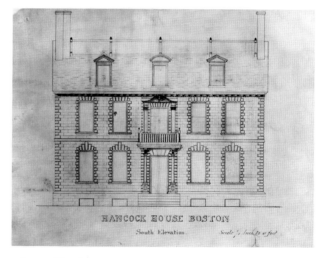

John Hubbard Sturgis, measured drawing of the facade of the John Hancock House, Boston, Mass., 1737

From this peculiarly "modern" perception was born the phenomenon of historicism—an interest in, and multifaceted representation of, the past. During the last quarter of the nineteenth century, a particularly American historicism emerged: the colonial revival movement. This cultural phenomenon encompassed a broad range of activities and produced a wide variety of objects, all of which made manifest a general fascination with the nation's past that had become widespread around the time of the centennial celebration of the War

THE COLONIAL REVIVAL AND MAINE

of Independence in 1876.[3] In that year, an international exposition held in Philadelphia's Fairmount Park not only championed American technological progress in the hundred years that had passed since the beginning of the Revolutionary War but also engendered a passion for all things "colonial." It is appropriate to place quotation marks around the word "colonial," for what was meant by it was any aspect of American culture that seemed to belong to the period before industrialization took hold, a process that became evident in the mid-nineteenth century, well after political independence had been won.

A few examples suggest the ubiquity of the colonial revival in the last decades of the nineteenth century. The Centennial Exposition, for instance, featured a "colonial kitchen" with a large open fireplace. The exhibit created the image of the cozy and cheerful colonial home, seemingly immune to the kinds of social and political conflicts, as well as economic changes, that were profoundly changing the world at that time. By 1876 open-hearth cooking had been replaced in most homes by the use of metal stoves, yet the visible fire and impressive dimensions of the hearth were displayed as testimony to what was nostalgically perceived to have been the warm and comfortable domesticity of premodern times.

The authors of fictional accounts of the Revolution and early years of the nation sparked the interest of the American public about the life and times of the colonial era. Perhaps the most influential of these authors was Henry Wadsworth Longfellow, who began to publish poems such as the much-loved and often memorized "Paul Revere's Ride" in the newly-founded *Atlantic Monthly* magazine in 1857. Interestingly, Longfellow's poetry often centered on buildings, the tangible reminders of the past. This was the case with his well-known "Tales of a Wayside Inn." In October 1862 Longfellow noted in his diary a trip he made with publisher James T. Fields to the old Red-Horse Tavern in Sudbury, Massachusetts, which became the model for the Wayside Inn. He recounted their approach, on a "delicious Indian-summer day," through a "lovely valley; the winding road shaded by grand old oaks before the house" to a "rambling, tumble-down old building, two hundred years old, and till now in the family of the Howes, who have kept an inn for one hundred and seventy-five years."[4] The very decrepitude of the building attracted Longfellow, as did its setting, which was notably wooded and rural. The

2

MAIN BUILDING,
INTERNATIONAL EXHIBITION.
1878.
FAIRMOUNT PARK   PHILADELPHIA.

Louis Abrun, International Exposition, Main Building, Philadelphia, Penn., 1876

inn evoked a sunny view of the past where human beings had traveled unhurriedly by winding roads and had lived in harmony with unspoiled nature. Writing at the time of the Civil War, Longfellow offered his readers images of a seemingly simpler and more harmonious time, responding to their need for escape from the appalling violence of the war and the sweeping changes that characterized the period more generally.

Longfellow's pilgrimage to Sudbury was paralleled by the trips made by historians, architects, antiquarians, and interested amateurs to places of historical significance. Among the most famous was Mount Vernon, the Virginia home of President George Washington. In 1859 the Mount Vernon Ladies' Association of the Union began a campaign to transform Mount Vernon *"from*

Hamilton House, South Berwick, circa 1787, with renovations and additions attributed to Little & Browne, 1899

what it is, to what it was."[5] The great national support their efforts were met with testifies to the continuing power of Washington's image and to the value of his achievements as a great military and political leader. The preservation of Mount Vernon inspired similar campaigns throughout the North and South. Beginning in the 1890s, the National Society of the Colonial Dames of America documented thousands of historic structures and supported the restoration of many as museum houses. In 1910 the Society for the Preservation of New England Antiquities, dedicated to restoring and maintaining examples of the region's historic architecture, was founded, followed in 1948 by a similar society on New York's Long Island. These institutions, together with countless local and state historical societies, undertook to restore and preserve the nation's colonial legacy.

As Longfellow anticipated in his appreciative account of the Sudbury inn, the public responded to the formal characteristics of older buildings quite apart from any knowledge of who had lived in them. The ramshackle appearance of the Howe's hostelry that attracted Longfellow would similarly draw architects, artists, and writers to modest vernacular structures that testified to the colonial past. Indeed, communities of artists grew up around places, especially on the East Coast, that had been left behind by modernization and that still possessed collections of old houses, churches, and other buildings. In New England there were many such enclaves, including Old Lyme, Connecticut, where the American Impressionist painter Childe Hassam settled for the summers just after 1900. There, and in nearby Cos Cob, he and his friends painted the vernacular buildings and landscapes that reflected the area's early history as an important maritime port.[6]

Artists' colonies also proliferated in the historic towns of northern New England. In Cornish, New Hampshire sculptor Augustus Saint-Gaudens, who summered there from 1885 on, and architect Charles Platt, who first visited the town in 1889, built summer residences and studios that drew other artists to the area.[7] In southern Maine, artists of both conservative and modernist predilections were drawn to the fishing village at Perkins Cove in Ogunquit, where they made paintings of the fishermen's white clapboard houses and shingled sheds.

Other students of colonial architecture sought out finer examples of eighteenth- and nineteenth-century American buildings in which the British and European academic traditions had been adapted to the colonial situation. Their research culminated in books and articles that described and reproduced the elements of colonial architecture. Through their publications, these antiquarian-architects made northern New England's historic architecture known to a national audience.[8]

One group of such architects, headquartered in Boston, brought about the revival of a specific type of colonial architecture—the classically inspired buildings constructed in northern New England from approximately 1780 to 1830. This architecture had originally been produced by carpenter-builders who drew particularly on the British neoclassical tradition of the seventeenth and eighteenth centuries. In general, American neoclassical buildings were constructed of wood—as opposed to the stone and brick commonly employed in England and on the Continent—and made prominent use of neoclassical details. Such elements included pilasters (especially at the corners of symmetrical building facades), Palladian windows, fan lights (over doorways), columned porches, and flush board siding that when painted gave the appearance of stone.

The neoclassical idiom had been most fully developed in America's cities, in the work of "gentleman architect" Charles Bulfinch (1763–1844) of Boston, for instance. Bulfinch's well-known designs, such as the Massachusetts State House of 1795 to 1798 and the three houses he designed on or near Beacon Hill for merchant Harrison Gray Otis between 1796 and 1806, inspired more modest versions along the seacoasts of Maine, New Hampshire, and elsewhere—in fact, anywhere there was a sizeable population of wealthy patrons.

Neoclassical architecture tended to be embraced in coastal New England by merchants and ships' captains, who played important roles in establishing international trade networks and in bringing knowledge of foreign cultures back to the United States. Although their houses were large and stylish, they were nonetheless considered, by virtue of their neoclassicism, restrained and elegant rather than ostentatious and vulgar. The words that the popular historical writer Mary Caroline Crawford attributed to the French Marquis de Chastellux during his visit to a Newburyport, Massachusetts house around the time of the Revolution fairly summarize later attitudes toward the homes of New England's mercantile elite: "The house is very handsome and well-furnished and everything breathes that air of magnificence accompanied by simplicity, which is only to be found among merchants."[9] The popular notion that the classical tradition promoted reason in design, that it offered a system to be mastered rather than inspiration for personal expression, made neoclassical buildings seem rational even when they represented extravagant expenditures.

From the 1870s onward, as colonial- and federal-period architecture became more familiar to architects and potential clients alike, neoclassical forms were introduced with increased frequency in new building. What began with the isolated inclusion of a few historicizing details during the last quarter of the nineteenth century became a wholesale appropriation of neoclassical forms and motifs by the time of the First World War.[10] The central essay contained in this book examines the processes by which northern New England's neoclassical architecture became familiar to architects and came to influence their new designs. Subsequent essays document the results of these architects' historical studies, as evidenced in the public and private buildings they constructed along the Maine coast.

At the center of this study are several architectural firms—Peabody & Stearns, Cabot & Chandler, and the practice of William Ralph Emerson—in which a fascination with colonial architecture was cultivated by the principals among a corps of draftsmen. These draftsmen, including William E. Barry and Arthur Little, contributed, in turn, to the colonial revival by publishing examples of early American architecture and by incorporating elements of these buildings into their own commissions.

Many of the commissions undertaken by the firms and their junior associates supported the creation of new resort towns in northern New England and especially along the Maine coast in the period following the Civil War. With the increased size of vessels requiring deeper harbors, the decline in wooden shipbuilding, and the shift of agriculture to the West, many New England port cities found themselves with outmoded facilities and a dearth of commercial activity.[11] The factory towns of Lewiston and Biddeford notwithstanding, many Maine communities came to rely increasingly on tourism as a source of economic activity. Many towns seized upon their rich histories as their greatest assets, enticing tourists to come to Maine not only to experience its rocky coast, unspoiled beaches, salty air, woods, and marshes but also its old seaports, with their rows of elegant houses and spired churches. A growing urban middle class embraced the romantic image of New England's storied coastal villages. Some came for the day; others stayed overnight in newly constructed hotels. Still others built houses and became long-term summer residents. Architects were called upon to produce designs for this new leisure class that were in keeping with both the state's natural environment and its historic architectural fabric. Wood sheathing was generally preferred for the new cottages and hotels. Shingles and clapboards stained gray or brown blended with the prevailing tones of the landscape, while historical details tied the new buildings to the old.

Reaching Maine's burgeoning resort communities was greatly facilitated in the late nineteenth century by improvements in transportation. Steamships carried vacationers from New York, Boston, and other cities to places as far away as Deer Isle, in Penobscot Bay, and Bar Harbor to the north. By century's end, railroads and trolleys criss-crossing the state made it possible to travel to even the most distant locales. As early as 1840, the Eastern Railroad provided passenger service from Boston up the North Shore to Kittery, Maine. Service to the beach towns of York County (Wells, Kennebunk, and Old Orchard among them) was provided from 1872 by the Boston and Maine Railroad (B&M), which had consolidated the lines built by many smaller railroad companies between 1835 and 1864.[12] As historian Dona Brown has demonstrated, the railroad companies played a major role in resort development. The B&M, for example, established the Boston and Kennebunkport Seashore Company, which built a hotel, casino, and boarding houses to entice summer visitors to travel by railroad to York County.[13] While some of these facilities had older buildings adapted for them, others required new purpose-built structures. The new casinos, hotels, and cottages often echoed the forms of the historic buildings whose charms the railroad builders clebrated.

Although the colonial revival as a conspicuous cultural movement began with the Centennial Exposition, its precise end is more difficult to date. In fact, it

Thomas Eaton, First Parish Church, Kennebunk, 1803

has been said more than once that the movement is not yet over. The ongoing pro-liferation of colonial-style residences in Maine generally substantiates that point of view. [14] It is fair to say, however, that the widespread enthusiasm for the colonial revival as an idiom for resort architecture diminished in the period between the two world wars, when another style became more widely accepted: modernism. In the postwar period especially, as more informal concepts of vacationing began to emerge and as the outmoded ark of the colonial revival cottage grew increasingly expensive to maintain, the simpler modern house became the norm.

The economic expansion of the late 1990s, combined with a growth in popular appreciation for historicist architecture, has created a favorable climate for the preservation of Maine's colonial-revival and shingle-style cottages today. Once again they are highly prized in the real estate market and sought out pre-cisely for such defining elements as their broad verandahs, natural building materials, and elaborate details (both inside and out). Almost unthinkably from the perspective of a few decades ago, these residences have not only been restored but even expanded as the average American house size has increased.

The colonial revival and shingle styles have also become the subjects of a revival themselves. In many Maine resort towns, as well as in year-round com-munities, the modest modern residences of the mid-twentieth century are increasingly being torn down to make way for new construction. The buildings that rise on these sites are almost uniformly historicist in character, adopting the gambrel roofs, Palladian windows, porches, and unpainted shakes associated with turn-of-the-century revival styles. Unfortunately, these new "super-sized shingle style" cottages (to borrow the wording of a recent real estate advertise-ment), with their preposterous combinations of mass-produced details, rarely achieve the graceful integration with the local architectural language and topo-graphical character that distinguished the best historicist residential buildings in Maine from the last quarter of the nineteenth century. Through their truly profound knowledge of historic buildings and their respectful approach to the landscape, late-nineteenth-century architects created an idiom that could well be a model for new construction. ❀

Map of the Kennebunks, 1872

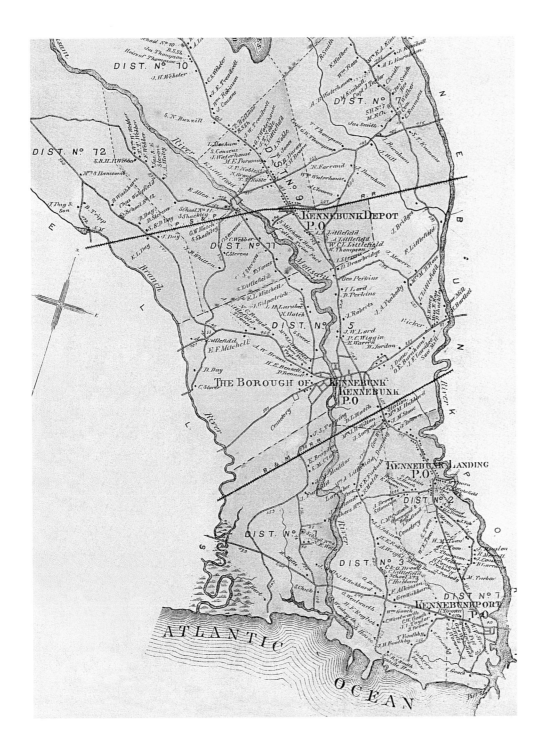

Kevin D. Murphy

PICTURESQUE AND REFINED:
THE COLONIAL REVIVAL IN MAINE

The Fairbanks House, Dedham, Mass., 1636, as it appeared in 1881

Yet, while picturesque effects add many charms to the old mansions, their distinguished and refined character still seems owing to careful rules and studied training in the orders and their details.[1]

SO WROTE ROBERT SWAIN PEABODY in 1878. The architect's words fold together two qualities that were often seen as mutually exclusive in design: irregular massing and classical discipline. The former was associated with vernacular buildings—modest one-story houses that had been added on to over time to form rambling, asymmetrical structures. The latter was thought to have originated in the temples and monuments of ancient Greece and Rome and to have been preserved principally in the work of Italian Renaissance architects. Architects and builders of the colonial and federal periods adapted the classical tradition to the requirements and conditions of North America. It was their neoclassical designs that attracted Peabody along with a group of other Boston architects, leading them to rediscover historic American architecture during the last quarter of the nineteenth century and use it to formulate a new architectural style.[2]

Despite the group's common interest in the architecture of the young nation, their affiliation was not through any one institution. They knew one another, worked together at times, and shared certain attitudes, although there were differences between them with respect to what drew them to neoclassical architecture. Robert Peabody, William Ralph Emerson, and Francis Chandler headed firms within which other, younger men worked. All three employed William E. Barry at one time or another. Peabody employed Arthur Little. Emerson was a great influence on John Calvin Stevens. Both Barry and Little worked in the firm of Cabot & Chandler. Draftsmen sometimes moved rapidly between firms and formed alliances with others as they established their own practices. Although many of these architects were members of the same professional organizations and cultural societies, they were never formally organized as a group.

William Ralph Emerson,
photograph, circa 1900

Robert Peabody (left), with
Francis W. Chandler (center)
and family, North Haven,
photograph, circa 1895

This book charts the emergence within this loose association of architects of a neoclassical revival through their publications and built works. It tells the story of a movement, comparable to many others of its time, that advocated a return to past ways of designing and making things rooted in a disgust with the results of contemporary production methods. This historicist impulse culminated in what have been retrospectively identified as overlapping movements, including the colonial revival, the Queen Anne movement, the arts-and-crafts movement, the design reform movement, and the aesthetic movement, among others. The buildings and interiors designed by the men discussed here display forms associated with most of these movements, but underlying all of their work was a concern with the legacy of neoclassical architecture. The term "colonial revival" underscores their general reliance on earlier American architectural styles.

Neoclassical architecture of the colonial and federal periods constituted a fragile legacy in the late nineteenth century. The pace and scope of environmental change in the preceding half-century must have impressed architects with the possibility that the physical record of early buildings could be completely obliterated. Architects who were born in the 1830s and 1840s came to their majority during the 1850s and 1860s, the decades that culminated in the Civil War. Their youths had been characterized by years of rapid industrialization in New England, and they were faced with vivid evidence of the roller-coaster economy of industrial capitalism with the Panic of 1873. Financial instability could undermine the ability of home owners to maintain their historic buildings. Furthermore, industrialization had contributed to urbanization around the mills of Boston, Lawrence, and Lowell, Massachusetts; Manchester, New Hampshire; and elsewhere. The density of buildings and populations in New England cities exacerbated social problems and natural disasters alike. Witness the Great Boston Fire of 1872, after which, "In the stead of noble buildings of granite and marble and brick were huge, giant walls, torn and ragged, and broken columns of stone and iron."[3] The fragility of the built environment as a result of all of these factors impressed young Boston architects and, in various ways, motivated them to contribute to the preservation of historic American architecture.

Early American architecture was not only lost to urban expansion and conflagrations but also became at times the casualty of changing tastes at mid-century.

This danger was recognized by Little in the preface to his 1878 book *Early New England Interiors*, in which he wrote that the sketches used as illustrations were "the result of a Summer's work, undertaken for my own pleasure and instruction, and also with the desire to preserve the relics of a style fast disappearing;—this disappearance owing partly to the perishable materials of the work, but chiefly to the national love of new things in preference to old."[4] Wood construction was susceptible to destruction by rot and flames but also by the fickle tastes of the growing consumer class. The complaint—voiced by countless domestic "reformers" in the second half of the nineteenth century—that mass production had led to a debasement of home furnishings had as its corollary the fear that many consumers were immune to the charms of earlier buildings. It was within this climate that, in print and in presentations to professional groups, Emerson, Peabody, Barry, and Little all asserted the attractions of earlier neoclassical architecture and its appropriateness as a model for new building.

John Calvin Stevens, sketch, circa 1930

For all of these architects there were safe havens from change: northern New England and Maine in particular. York, the Kennebunks, Portland, and other port cities to the north preserved examples of colonial- and federal-period architecture and, by the mid-1870s, afforded opportunities to build using new designs that harmonized with the old.

The reasons that rural northern New England preserved what had been lost elsewhere were not obscure. The Embargo Act of 1807 and the War of 1812 brought an end to what had been a recent and relatively short-lived mercantile boom. Some formerly prosperous southern Maine port towns like York lost population in the second half of the nineteenth century. The decline after mid-century in the building of wooden sailing vessels and the obsolescence of smaller ports as ships increased in size brought economic stagnation or worse. The silver lining of economic depression was architectural preservation; many Maine towns were spared the desecration of their surviving colonial and early nineteenth-century buildings by the sheer lack of financial means to alter or build them anew.[5] It is more than a coincidence that the men who would shape the historicist architectural culture of the late-nineteenth century came mostly from rural northern New England.

Celebrated by the architects were those buildings that represented the period prior to the advent of large-scale industrial production in New England. Peabody, Emerson, Little, Barry, and others admired the generation of houses built just before the large-scale introduction of mass-produced building materials like dimensional lumber and machine-cut nails. In contrast to these architects' own time, when "the jig-saw and the lathe were prolifically serving [an] ostentatious, *nouveau-riche* clientele,"[6] in the federal period and earlier, owners had judiciously embraced handicraft, guided by a sense of classical restraint that builders had internalized (or so it was thought). For some late nineteenth-century critics, earlier domestic architecture was more tasteful than contemporary houses.

In fact, eighteenth-century American builders often relied on published neo-classicist designs rather than on innate good taste. The broad dissemination of knowledge about classical architecture had essentially begun when British anti-quarians James Stuart and Nicholas Revett surveyed the classical buildings of Athens between 1751 and 1754 and published the first volume of their drawings, based on measurements of Greek monuments, in 1762. Two years later the influential architect Robert Adam (1728–1792) published drawings he had made, with the assistance of draftsmen, of the remains of the Palace of the Emperor Diocletian in Split, Croatia. The British focused their attention not only on the remaining buildings of antiquity but also on Italian Renaissance interpretations of the classical tradition, especially as developed in the works of Andrea Palladio (1508–1580). This northern Italian architect inspired neoclassical designs by British architects such as Sir Christopher Wren (1632–1723), James Gibbs (1682–1754), and William Chambers (1723–1796).

British Palladian designs were known in North America through a variety of publications, including those of William Pain (circa 1730–1790).[7] The British author exerted an important influence on, among other American architects, Asher Benjamin (1773–1845), whose series of books, beginning with the *Country Builder's Assistant* of 1797, were widely read.[8] The neoclassical buildings of southern Maine often reflected local builders' reliance on the published designs of Benjamin and others, or on the works of Boston architects who were taken with British Palladianism and Adamesque neoclassicism, especially Charles Bulfinch (1763–1844). Chief

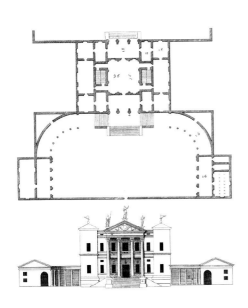

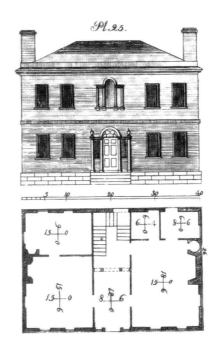

Andrea Palladio, Villa for Count Oleardo and Count Theodoro de Thieni at Cigogna, from *The Four Books of Architecture*, 1570

Asher Benjamin, *The Country Builder's Assistant* (1798), plate 29

among the interpreters of neoclassicism in southern Maine was Thomas Eaton (active 1794–1831), who designed a series of impressive houses for members of the local elite that would become of great interest to later generations of architects.[9]

ESTABLISHING THE COLONIAL REVIVAL

Certain Boston architects were influential in the development along the Maine coast of a historically inflected style for public buildings, hotels, and "cottages," or summer retreats, often with multiple stories, formal living and dining areas, numerous bedrooms accommodating frequent guests, and even separate quarters for the servants who accompanied their employers on vacation. William Ralph Emerson and Robert Swain Peabody both established architectural firms after the Civil War in which an appreciation for New England's architectural patrimony flourished. The two men emphasized the importance of recording earlier architecture by encouraging their draftsmen to draw old buildings and argued for the saliency of eighteenth- and early nineteenth-century architecture as models for new design.

Of the two, Peabody took the more public role in advocating a colonial revival. In "A Talk about 'Queen Anne'" delivered to the Boston Society of Architects on April 6, 1877, the architect articulated a vision for an American version of the British Queen Anne style.[10] The talk was formulated as a response to the sentiment, expressed at a previous meeting of the society, that the Queen Anne was "a movement of no account," "a whim of a few people, and one that we need not interest ourselves about."[11] Peabody identified British architect Richard Norman Shaw as the leader of the movement, one of the principal features of which was the adaptation of "any eccentricity in general design that one can suppose would have occurred to designers one hundred and fifty or two hundred years ago." In an age of warring historical styles, from the classical to the medieval and beyond, Peabody defended the relevance of the Queen Anne:

> To those who do believe in revivals, "Queen Anne" is a very fit importation into our offices. There is no revival so little of an affectation on our soil, as that of the beautiful work of the Colonial days. Its quiet dignity and quaintness and elegance, always attract us. It is our legitimate field for imitation, and we have much of it to study right in our own neighborhood. In fact, any one who in summer drives over the ancient turnpike from Hingham to Plymouth will not only pass through a beautiful country full of old homesteads, but will find the sunflowers still nodding behind the gambrel-roofed houses that line the road through Queen Anne's corner.[12]

In this passage, Peabody slips between discussing English Queen Anne and American colonial architecture. The slippage is significant, for it suggests the equation Peabody drew between the two sources of inspiration available to his contemporaries. In other articles he further developed his understanding of the similarities between the two styles. The underlying commonality he saw was an innate classicism, to be observed in the seventeenth- and eighteenth-century buildings of both England and the United States.

In an October 1877 article published in the *American Architect and Building News*, Peabody again addressed the Queen Anne movement. He discussed the "Georgian houses of New England" and reported on the philosophy embraced by English Queen Anne designers. Peabody explained their fascination with the seventeenth century on the basis of the period's unselfconscious way of using classicism. "Classical detail as introduced in Renaissance days," he wrote, "had become completely naturalized, and gradually it had ceased to be used in a servile way, or with great regard for precedent; but it simply made things seem attractive without much thought of purity of style, or style at all."[13] Similarly, Peabody maintained, "we find in the Georgian days [in the North American colonies] men working without thought of style, simply, delicately, beautifully." He further elaborated, "in the old houses, we find a classical detail universally used, the common language of every carpenter, and treated freely with regard only to comfort, cosiness or stateliness." For both English and American architects, Peabody inferred that it was most appropriate to revive the style from a period in which there had been no self-conscious awareness of style and in which instead the classical tradition undergirded every aspect of building. Thus the strategy of Queen Anne designers pointed the way forward at a moment in which—according to Peabody, at least—Americans were "past the battle of styles."[14] In a subsequent article, Peabody made the point even more bluntly, asserting that in the colonial period "the use of classical detail was universally agreed to, and the orders were naturally used by every carpenter."[15]

As previously suggested, this universal agreement to incorporate classicism had not been the result of New England builders having internalized a knowledge of classical principles but instead had emerged from a reliance on architectural pattern books and primers that presented examples of how the classical language of architecture could be adapted to building relatively small-scale, wood-frame buildings in North America. According to Peabody, the books of Asher Benjamin, Batty Langley, and others were important for their strict adherence to the classical tradition: "Almost all the designing found in these volumes is founded on the study of the orders, which is throughout held as almost synonymous with the study of architecture."[16]

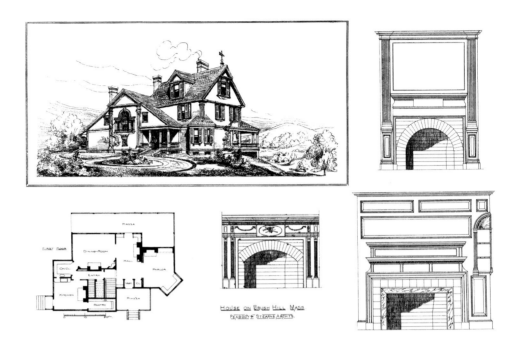

Peabody & Stearns, the John W. Denny House, Milton, Mass., 1878

The liability of relying on all of this classical rigor was the potential for monotony: "The later [federal-period] and richer mansions were large and square, and with so little detail outside, that one built now would, without the benefit of age, seem unpleasantly angular and box-like."[17] Thus Peabody maintained alongside the classicist sensibility an appreciation for the picturesque, which he perceived in two buildings in particular:

> The old Fairbanks house at Dedham, partly early with high-pitched roof and partly later with gambrel roof, forms a most picturesque pile; and so does the scattered [Wentworth-Coolidge] house at Little Harbor, with gables at different heights, and floors at different levels; while the council-chamber wing runs off at an uncalled for angle with the main building, that would delight Mr. Norman Shaw.[18]

Around 1878 Peabody designed the John W. Denny House in Milton, Massachusetts, which incorporates neoclassical elements into a domestic architectural conception

Arthur Little, *Early New England Interiors* (1878), title page

that comes directly from the Queen Anne movement.[19] On the exterior, the facade's two-story pilasters and Palladian window announce the design's neoclassical inspiration, while the gabled kitchen and entry block that projects toward the street and a window bay that juts out from the corner of the parlor relieve the boxy mass of the house and create what Peabody would have deemed a "picturesque" profile. On the interior, the plan is equally Queen Anne in inspiration, having a "living hall" of the type popularized by Shaw with a large fireplace and inglenook at the end opposite the entrance. At the same time, one of the mantelpieces is flanked by paired classical columns and is ornamented with a frieze containing swags reminiscent of federal-period mantels.

Peabody's architectural temperament, which accommodated Queen Anne "eccentricity" within a broader preference for classicism, evidently infused the work of his draftsmen.[20] One image makes the point: the title page of Little's *Early New England Interiors*, which was in preparation at just the time that Peabody's articles were being published, possesses both qualities.[21] At the center of the page is

Arthur Little, renovation to
76 Beacon Street, Boston,
circa 1890

Richard Norman Shaw, Old
Swan House, London,
1875–77

the Wentworth-Coolidge House. Little's drawing, with its inconsistent use of perspective, only accentuates the "uncalled for" angles and idiosyncratic character of the mansion. Borders and a vignette of sunflowers—a favorite motif of the English Queen Anne movement—frame the central image. At the upper left corner, seemingly laid over the rest of the page, is a detail drawing of a house facade featuring a Georgian doorway framed by classical elements. The open door provides an inviting glimpse of the stair within. The affinities begin to suggest how Peabody and his draftsmen collectively formulated a new historicist aesthetic that was indebted to both English and American precedents.

One of Little's built projects further underscores the centrality of Shaw's work to Peabody and his draftsmen. Around 1890 Little altered the granite rowhouse at 76 Beacon Street in Boston, one in a group of six begun by the Mount Vernon Proprietors in 1828. To the stark Greek-revival facade Little added first-story bay and second-story oriel windows, both elements clearly modeled on Shaw's Old Swan House in London of 1875–77.[22]

The congruence between Little's and Peabody's architectural viewpoints (articulated in drawings and writings, respectively) is not surprising given that the two men had explored the historic buildings in the area of Portsmouth, New Hampshire together during the summer of 1877. Nor is it startling to discover that like-minded architects conducted similar sketching trips in an effort to document northern New England's early buildings: The New York architects Charles F. McKim (Peabody's colleague during their student years at the Ecole des Beaux-Arts in Paris), William R. Mead, William Bigelow, and Stanford White made a celebrated journey that included Marblehead, Salem, and Newburyport, in addition to Portsmouth, in the very same year. Mead later attributed the classical leanings of the firm to that trip.[23] Peabody's other colleague from Paris, Francis Chandler, also formed an architectural office in which colonial revival sensibilities were fostered. Chandler, along with McKim and Peabody, gained from their European training many things, not the least of which was a commitment to architectural history.[24] The course of study at the Ecole des Beaux-Arts emphasized the continuing relevance of the classical tradition as well as the necessity of drawing examples of historic styles as a way of understanding them. Thus, when the former Ecole students

Peabody & Stearns, the Pierre Lorillard House, or the Breakers, Newport, R.I., 1877–78

returned to the United States, they set out to document examples of earlier American architecture in drawings.

DEVELOPING THE NEOCLASSICAL REVIVAL

Late in his life, Robert Peabody likened the series of draftsmen who moved through the firm he headed with John Goddard Stearns to a circus parade, not because of any clownishness on the part of the young men but because their numbers had been so large and the stream seemingly unending. Peabody recalled:

> On returning from Paris [in 1870], Stearns and I began a busy life together, which has had few interruptions for this long period. Many changes have occurred since the

days when our comrades, the two [Francis and Theophilus] Chandlers and [Henry] Richards and Willie Barry and [Warren] Briggs came in to help us on our first jobs.[25]

The relationship between Peabody and his draftsmen—or "comrades," as he called them—appears to have been mutually beneficial: He taught them about architectural practice, and they contributed in important ways to the firm's designs.

Maine native William E. Barry brought his long-standing fascination with historic architecture to the firm. The first project he is thought to have assisted with is the Nathan Matthews House in Newport, Rhode Island of 1871–72. It is also likely that he had a hand in the design of the tobacco magnate Pierre Lorillard's cottage, the Breakers, of 1877–78, also in Newport. In addition to some Queen Anne features, the Breakers incorporates certain colonial motifs, which suggests that at that moment, the firm was beginning to emerge as a center for the investigation of early American architecture.

William E. Barry, photograph, circa 1870

Peabody's passion for colonial architecture was probably something that his draftsmen embraced because of their own previous experiences. Barry, for instance, had developed an interest in early American architecture as a young child.[26] His first independent commission—the 1872–73 renovation of his mother's house—also showed his appreciation for federal-period architecture in its use of neoclassical elements such as columns supporting a classical frieze with triglyphs.[27] By designing his additions "in the old style,"[28] Barry demonstrated his respect for the original 1803–04 building. He created an important colonial revival project—one that predated by three years the Centennial celebration of 1876 and the more general appreciation of "colonial" architecture that it engendered. These additions also predated Peabody's public call for a revival style based on historic American precedent. It is likely that Peabody's architectural opinions were formulated in dialogue with Barry, whose fondness for the federal period took shape as a child in Kennebunk and was nurtured in Emerson's office.

In the mid-1870s, Barry traveled to England and studied examples of Queen Anne architecture first hand. During the same period, he also studied historic architecture in the United States. His knowledge of colonial and federal-period neoclassicism is evident in his many drawings of the salient features of buildings

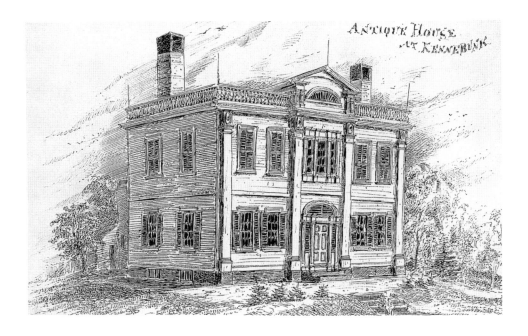

William E. Barry, William Lord House, Kennebunk, 1801 (top), and Coventry Hall, York, 1794–96 (bottom), from *Pen Sketches of Old Houses* (1874)

"Our ship's jibboom pointing towards Liverpool," drawing from the sketchbook of Willaim E. Barry, circa 1872

from these periods, collected in the 1874 book *Pen Sketches of Old Houses.*[29] Included in the slim volume are numerous images of neoclassical houses in southern Maine and drawings of buildings from a number of American cities that Barry visited in the early 1870s, from the William Lord House in Kennebunk, Maine of about 1800 and the Aspinwall House in Brookline, Massachusetts of 1803 to Mount Pleasant in Philadelphia of 1761 and a nineteenth-century sod tomb in New Orleans.[30]

The letters Barry wrote to family members at home during his extensive travels throughout the United States and abroad make it clear that the architect was well aware of the competition between revival styles that had been ongoing in Europe since the mid-century. They also make unambiguous Barry's preference for neoclassicism. In Paris, he admired Jacques-Germain Soufflot's eighteenth-century Church of Sainte-Geneviève (later the Panthéon), with its dome and columned portico, but distained the Gothic cathedral of Notre-Dame. In London he preferred Wren's St. Paul's Cathedral, inspired by the renaissance and baroque forms of St. Peter's in Rome, to Charles Barry and A. W. N. Pugin's recently completed Neogothic Houses of Parliament.[31] He made the revealing observation, "The town architecture in England does not seem to be on so large a scale as at home. All of stone or brick and tile and slate, vines, with antiquated oriel windows, and carving, projecting second stories and odd dormer windows. There are no white wooden houses."[32] Clearly, Barry was noting the absence of the austere wood-frame buildings of the colonial and federal periods in Maine and other parts of New England that were familiar to him.

For Barry Europe possessed a worthy tradition of classical architecture and demonstrated in its recent buildings the full variety of revival styles.[33] The Continent for him was a kind of museum of preindustrial ways of life, the loss of

Washington's Retreat
near Philadelphia.

Carpenter's Hall
Philadelphia.

Souvenir of the Centennial Exposition, Fairmont Park, Philadelphia, 1876

which he lamented. In a letter dated August 20, 1872, Barry described an experience he had had in Interlaken, Switzerland:

> I heard a pounding all about and could not tell what it meant, until I went about and
> found it to come from the farmers, who with their wives and women folk, were beating
> the grain on their barn floors with flails. I looked on with delight. "Good," said I to
> myself, "here is a people who do not change. This is as it was in New England once."[34]

The Continent's rural pockets preserved, as did parts of northern New England,
images of a way of life untouched by modernization. For Barry, as for Peabody, Europe
provided models for the development of an American historicism.

In addition to contributing to the design of Peabody's early colonial revival
houses, Barry also assisted Arthur Little with his first independent commission,

Arthur Little, the Cliffs, Manchester, Mass., 1879

Page from a sketchbook of William E. Barry, no date

a house called the Cliffs in Manchester, Massachusetts, of 1879.[35] The centennial year, during which Little and Barry worked in the office of Peabody & Stearns, was, of course, a key one for anybody interested in historic American architecture. The Centennial Exposition, held in Philadelphia's Fairmount Park, created unprecedented public awareness of the nation's architectural legacy. In the following year Peabody and Little, both of whom had likely perused Barry's *Pen Sketches of Old Houses* and heard the architect extol the virtues of northern New England's neoclassical architecture, would themselves make a sketching trip to Portsmouth and its environs.[36]

As is plain from this discussion, it is impossible to attribute the growth of a colonial revival sensibility among Boston architects to a single individual. To do so would perhaps be to fail to recognize an atmosphere of collaboration that seems to have prevailed in the offices of many accomplished designers. Peabody, for example, while taking a vocal, personal role in the advocacy of the colonial revival, clearly valued the contributions of his draftsmen as well. Barry's work inside and outside of Peabody's office offers a unique opportunity to observe how one member of a firm built upon the work of his colleagues and mentors. Similarly, Little's artistic development and aesthetic sensibilities benefited from his association with Peabody's office and also with various family members and friends.

The drawings of Salem, Massachusetts houses Little published in his *Early New England Interiors* were made under the supervision of Henry Fitz Gilbert Waters, a Salem antiquarian and collector. Little may have been introduced to Waters through his uncle Clarence Cook, the prominent New York art critic who knew Waters's collection and who published the influential book *The House Beautiful* in 1878.[37] Interestingly, Cook's call for the reform of domestic furnishings and a return to certain historical precedents in design appeared in the very year that Little published his drawings of early house interiors. Between 1876 and 1878, Little was thus immersed in historicism through both his personal and professional associations. Like Barry, Little was privileged enough to have entry into sophisticated architectural and cultural circles. Both men synthesized the historical concerns of those around them as they contributed to a growing colonial revival in Boston.

THE MEANINGS OF AMERICAN NEOCLASSICISM

The preference for neoclassical architecture over the "shocking mongrels" of other historical styles competing for prominence in the nineteenth century might be considered an esoteric aesthetic matter if it were not for the larger significance that the classical tradition was thought to have had. In different ways, the architects who were at the center of the colonial revival in Boston attached an importance to their use of neoclassicism that went beyond strictly architectural considerations. For each of these men, the selection of colonial- and federal-period neoclassicism as a style for study and emulation constituted a response to certain social, political, and economic conditions of the late nineteenth century, particularly those that stemmed from industrialization.

In *The House Beautiful*, Cook vehemently objected to "the habit of over-ornamenting everything":

> It is not merely that we over-ornament; where ornament is advisable at all this is a natural enough fault to fall into, but we ornament a thousand things that ought not to be ornamented. It is hard to find an object of merchandise to-day that has not ornament (so called) of some kind stuck or fastened upon it.[38]

This was an objection voiced by many critics to the mass-produced objects marketed to middle-class consumers during the second half of the nineteenth century. Especially for upper-class observers, the advent of industrial production had led to a regrettable proliferation of overly decorative consumer goods and a consequent debasement of taste and craftsmanship. Edith Wharton and Ogden Codman, Jr., for example, wrote in their 1897 *The Decoration of Houses*, "the substitution of machine for hand-work has made possible the unlimited reproduction of works of art; and the resulting demand for cheap knick-knacks has given employment to a multitude of untrained designers having nothing in common with the *virtuoso* of former times."[39]

There were many responses to the perception that the factory production of household goods had made the middle-class home into an arena for the display of vulgar taste and poorly made furnishings. William Morris and his call for a return to preindustrial production methods with the arts-and-crafts movement

Frank Wallis, "Mantel Parlor 'Working Woman's Bureau'" and "Mantel in the Office of Mr. Arthur Little Archt.," drawing, circa 1900

constituted one such response, and the aesthetic movement—with which Cook is often associated—was another. Cook and similarly minded critics, architects, crafts-people, and artists advocated interiors furnished with a wide variety of objects from various cultures but all united by the integrity of their design and production. The preference for colonial- and federal-style neoclassical design stemmed from a similar perception that the buildings and furnishings of those periods were based on a classical tradition that was rational, dignified, and tasteful.

Among the architects who made this point in writing was Frank Wallis (1860–1929), an Eastport, Maine native who worked for Cabot & Chandler between 1876 and 1885. He subsequently joined Peabody & Stearns, where he stayed for about two years, before moving to New York and the office of Richard Morris Hunt. Wallis evidently knew Barry, who was also with Cabot & Chandler (from 1879 until the mid-1880s). He was apparently also friendly with Little, as he published a drawing of a neoclassical mantelpiece in Little's office in the *American Architect and Building News*.[40] Wallis's drawing of Salem fence posts suggests that he and Little may have had mutual acquaintances in the North Shore city. Wallis began publishing on the topic of American architecture about a decade after Barry and Little (he was substantially younger than they). In his 1887 *Old Colonial Architecture and Furniture*, he most often chose to represent architecture that had "for its foundation the classic of Palladio and Vignola" or "the influence of Sir Christopher Wren and the Adams Brothers,"[41] thus underscoring the continuity between European, British, and American neoclassicism.

In later writings Wallis asserted more forcefully the superiority of American neoclassicism as the basis of modern architecture. For the author, colonial architecture carried with it aristocratic associations. In a 1909 article in *Home and Garden* entitled "What and Why is Colonial Architecture?" Wallis claimed, "For a gentleman of taste, for all of discernment, the Colonial is the only fitting environment.... This type of house represents dignity, education, cultivation... as no other style devised by man can do." Within a colonial environment, Wallis believed the "kiddies" would absorb "unconsciously a keener appreciation of the finer things in life."[42]

In a book published a year later, Wallis explained that part of the value of colonial architecture derived from its association with New England's settlers, "humble but sturdy folk," each of whom had fled religious persecution and started life in the New World with no more than a loom, axe, and flint-lock. The stalwart settlers had invested their houses with meaning, and these buildings continued to reverberate with historical associations: "I myself have measured, sketched and studied the old houses, often with a strong stirring of emotion, being only one generation removed from this type."[43] For Wallis neo-classical American architecture of the eighteenth century was recommended for reuse by its design integrity and by its association with settlers whom he perceived as superior to his contemporaries. He summarized: "This is why the 'Georgian' period appeals to us. It is human and direct, and a true utilitarian expression of needs, and is therefore artistic and of value in the development of our modern styles."[44]

The idea that colonial architecture was an appropriate model for new building was commonplace by the first decade of the twentieth century, as is evidenced by the legions of "colonial" houses built around the United States in the decades leading up to the First World War. What is most significant about Wallis's argument, for our purposes, is that it grew out of his experience working for Peabody & Stearns and Cabot & Chandler, and with other architects who had northern New England roots. Barry and Little were less prolific writers than Wallis, but they likely helped to shape their younger colleague's view of the relationship between colonial society and neoclassical architecture.

The most developed and politically progressive rationale for the use of neo-classicism among the architects who practiced in southern Maine was produced by architectural partners John Calvin Stevens and Albert Winslow Cobb in 1888. The book they published jointly but which was written by Cobb, *Examples of American Domestic Architecture*, included plates illustrating their work. Most is in the shingle style, although around the time of the dissolution of their partnership in 1891 it had become more neoclassical in feeling. Cobb wrote scathingly on the topic of contemporary European architecture:

> The magnificent buildings of their aristocratic quarters, so exciting our emulation, have been built with inadequate recompense to their common workmen, so heavily

MAINE NO SHANTY TOWN TO BOSTON HERALD

The cartoon, shown here, was published in the Boston Herald, October 6, as a result of local controversy as to the suitability of the architecture of Boston's log cabin information building on the Common. Staff artist Dahl compares Boston's information office to Maine's Kittery Information Center of the Publicity Bureau. Our thanks to Dahl and to the Herald for "pointing with pride" to the way we do things here in Maine.

"Maine No Shanty Town to Boston Herald," *Maine Publicity Bureau News*, circa 1955

taxed and scantily paid. Their vaunted Art, in decorating a few sumptuous buildings, has often despoiled the homes of the populace.[45]

Cobb rejected any historical style based on the emulation of a period of political and social oppression, such as the French Rococo, which "expresses fittingly the character of that mad fever of voluptuous tyranny, which reached its height just before the awful corrective outbreak of the French people" of the French Revolution. Conversely, "whenever the democratic spirit was earliest developed and most marked, there the work done by our Carpenter-Architects of the colonial and Early National times exhibits most of pure beauty." Thus, "this 'Old Colonial' style, based on the Classic Orders, is particularly well adapted to domestic work."[46]

In both their studies of surviving colonial architecture and in their designs for new buildings in the Kennebunks and surrounding areas, the architects associated with Boston's colonial revival contributed to the establishment of a visual identity for New England, and for Maine in particular. The degree to which federal-period neoclassicism had become tied to northern New England's identity can be judged by John Howard Stevens's project for the Maine Publicity Bureau in York of 1929. For a narrow triangular site at the intersection of Route 1 and the road to historic York Village, Stevens chose to design a version of a late-eighteenth–century Cape Cod–style house with a three-bay facade and a centered entrance, flanked by a federal-style doorway. The most outstanding neoclassical features of the building were its gable-end parapet walls and its eyebrow windows wreathed in carved leaves and set in a flush-board frieze. These elements transformed a modest domestically scaled building into an image of architectural sophistication.

Maine's several neoclassical tourist information offices received some regional publicity when in 1955 controversy erupted over a log cabin information booth erected on Boston Common. A cartoon in the *Boston Herald* juxtaposed the cabin—which perhaps played upon the popular association between log construction and frontier culture—with the classically detailed Kittery tourist office and bore the caption, "They should *see* the kind of information booths there are in the 'wilds' of Maine." Founded in 1922, by which time the state's architectural legacy had been well published, and imitated, in growing resort communities, the Maine Publicity Bureau chose not to underscore its association with untamed natural landscapes but instead to emphasize its historical association with the classical tradition.

BUILDING MAINE'S RESORTS

By the 1920s Maine had become well known as a place not only of both natural beauty but also of historical interest. Designs for new resorts along the Maine coastline that occupied architects associated with the colonial revival were the result of a veritable explosion in travel, especially among members of the growing middle class, which began in the mid-nineteenth century. Summer visitors to the region abounded. While ante-bellum New England had been considered "the home of the most modern technological and social innovations of [its] day," in the second half of the century, as historian Dona Brown observes, "tourists began to perceive the region very differently. Increasingly, New England appeared to visitors as though it were a kind of museum, a storehouse for a whole collection of old-fashioned ways of being, of old-fashioned values and beliefs."[47] Some architects capitalized on this perception by designing resort architecture for the Maine coast that emphasized the historical interest of the place. From Kittery Point in the south to Bar Harbor and points north, architects fashioned a colonial revival aesthetic for many of the watering places created to cater to middle-class and wealthy tourists.

The development of Kennebunk and Kennebunkport as summer destinations typifies the emergence of resort areas in Maine. It began with the 1872 incorporation of the Sea Shore Company, which purchased a large tract of land running from the fishing village of Cape Porpoise at the north to the southern end of Kennebunk Beach. In between these two points were acres of open land ripe for development into numerous small cottage lots. Just three years later, in 1875, Samuel Adams Drake observed of Kennebunkport,

It is a queer old place, or rather was, before it became translated into a summer resort: but now silk jostles homespun, and for three months in the year it is invaded by an army of pleasure-seekers, who ransack its secret places, and after taking their fill of the sea and shore, flee before the first frosts of autumn.[48]

Henry Paston Clark, Breakwater Court (now the Colony Hotel), Kennebunkport, 1914

Beginning in the early 1870s, some summer residents built their own cottages. Other visitors stayed in large hotels, the first of which was constructed in 1873, or in smaller guest houses.

The rolling terrain and dramatic shoreline of Cape Arundel, between Cape Porpoise and the north side of the Kennebunk River, attracted cottage and hotel builders, beginning with William Heyer of Boston in 1874. Among the architects who were active at Cape Arundel was John Calvin Stevens, who designed a number of shingle-clad houses adorned with colonial details, which blended gracefully with the landscape. Boston architect Henry Paston Clark (1853–1927) also built cottages there as well as the prominent Breakwater Court (now, the Colony Hotel) in 1914. The historic village of Kennebunkport, near the mouth of the Kennebunk River, boasted a collection of neoclassical houses, some of which were sold to summer residents or transformed into businesses serving the resort

Maine Street, Kennebunkport, circa 1890

community. Emerson made substantial additions to the Nathaniel Lord House for summer use.[49] He also designed two shingled cottages at Cape Arundel in the late 1880s that included some neoclassical elements.[50] To the south of the river stretches Kennebunk Beach, where cottage lots were for sale as early as 1866; major construction, however, did not take place until the mid- to late 1870s. At the south end of Kennebunk Beach, Hartley Lord developed a spit of land originally known as Two Acres (now called Lord's Point), beginning in 1873; Barry's family connection with Lord, who was his uncle, brought him some commissions at Lord's Point, including the Kate Lord and Colonel Harris cottages, the latter just to the north of the point.[51] To the south of Lord's Point, on the south side of the Mousam River, Charles Parsons and his family built a number of summer residences along Hart's Beach, also in the early 1870s; at Parson's Beach, as it later became known, Barry designed several cottages, some of which drew upon federal-period neoclassicism.[52]

Maine was not unique among the New England states possessing maritime pasts that needed to rebuild their economies through tourism at the close of the nineteenth century. Places like Newport, Rhode Island and Nantucket Island, Massachusetts also fit this paradigm. Newport was far more fashionable and celebrated than any Maine resort, with the possible exception of Bar Harbor. Yet the significance of Maine's role in the colonial revival movement seems to have been surprisingly large given its small population and largely rural character. The state's historic buildings became well known nationally, and a substantial number of Maine men became important in Boston architectural circles in the last quarter of the century. Moreover, if Maine's resorts did not approach Newport's in terms of the ostentation of their cottages, that may have actually enhanced the significance of the colonial revival to the design of summer houses in the Pine Tree State. "Real" colonial houses were small in scale, and even very modest vernacular examples from the seventeenth and eighteenth centuries provided useful models for cottage designers. Finally, the synergism between shingle- and colonial revival–style architecture and Maine's landscape was arguably unique. The state's coast is thousands of miles long, extended by many coves and bays and varied by sandy beaches, estuaries, and jagged rock outcroppings. In the hands of talented designers, colonial revival cottages fit this special setting through their organic and picturesque qualities, which echoed the forms and textures and colors of the land itself. By visually relating the summer cottages and new year-round houses to the buildings that already defined Maine's coastal towns, architects fit their designs to the place.

The Boston architects who trained in the city's historicist firms during the 1870s and 1880s were united by their interest in the refined architecture of the colonial and federal periods. Their careers brought them to the Kennebunks and subsequently to surrounding towns. Their designs for new buildings in the spirit of the old set a standard for later architects.

Cottage owners came to Maine precisely because it was different from the cities where they spent the majority of their time. The designs that well-to-do summer visitors commissioned from architects within the state and beyond emphasized their conceptions of the place as one where history was apparent in the numerous surviving old buildings and where the natural environment was relatively unspoiled. Those urbanites who commissioned Maine cottages from the architects they knew in the places where they lived in the winter, or who patronized one of the well-known designers practicing in Maine's seacoast resorts, supported—however unconsciously—the development of colonial revival architecture. Members of Maine's year-round communities also contributed to the colonial revival as they built museums, libraries, and primary residences that made visual reference to the surviving architecture of earlier periods.

The historicist movement that began in the aftermath of the Civil War with Robert Peabody's and William Ralph Emerson's pleas to respect and make use of the architecture of early New England had by the start of the First World War become a national cultural phenomenon. In the intervening decades, the New England landscape had been irrevocably altered by industrialization, urbanization, and suburbanization. Resorts came to occupy large swaths of what had formerly been agricultural lands in the most picturesque parts of the region. Such thoroughgoing and rapid change stimulated vigorous efforts to recover and preserve New England's history, especially as it was made material in buildings. Possessing associations with what was imagined to have been the tasteful, hard-working, and prosperous merchant class of the late-eighteenth and early-nineteenth centuries, Maine's early neoclassical architecture provided an appealing visual language for later builders. Supplied with a set of forms firmly rooted in America's fabled past, the architects of the colonial revival attempted to excise the excesses of mid-century mass-produced architecture and created a new, if somewhat familiar, national style. ❧

William Ralph Emerson, Rock Ledge Cottage, Kennebunkport, circa 1895

William E. Barry, Kate Lord Cottage, Lord's Point, Kennebunk Beach, circa 1890

Bangor

Bath

Saco

Kennebunk

Kennebunkport

Kennebunk Beach

South
Berwick

York

C O A S T   O F

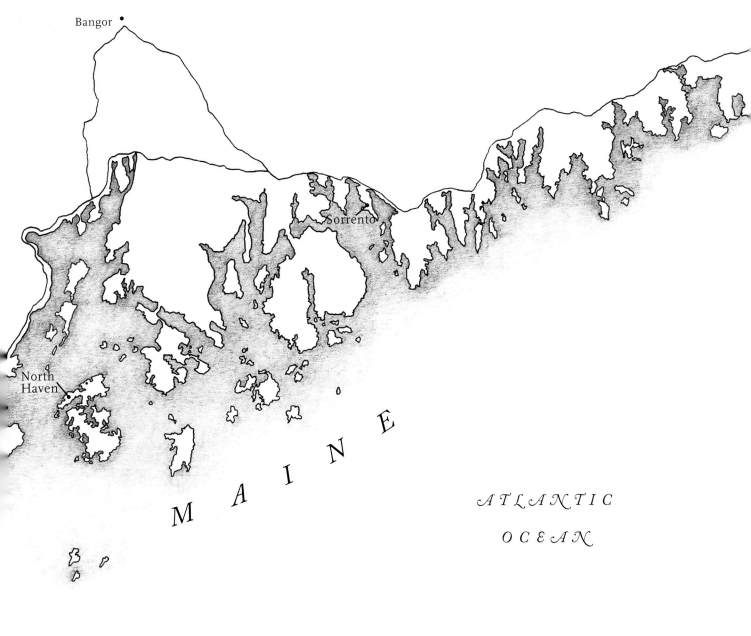

Bangor

Sorrento

North
Haven

M A I N E

ATLANTIC

OCEAN

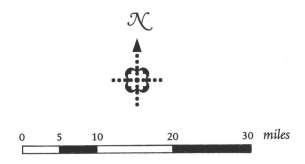

N

0   5   10   20   30   miles

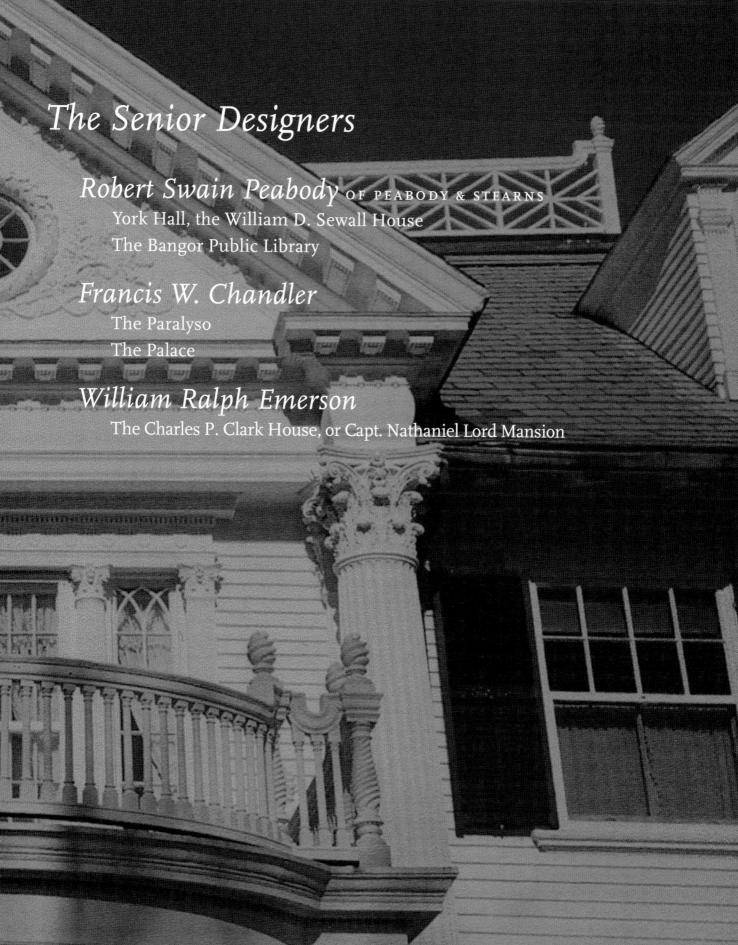

The Senior Designers

Robert Swain Peabody OF PEABODY & STEARNS
York Hall, the William D. Sewall House
The Bangor Public Library

Francis W. Chandler
The Paralyso
The Palace

William Ralph Emerson
The Charles P. Clark House, or Capt. Nathaniel Lord Mansion

Robert Swain Peabody OF PEABODY & STEARNS

ROBERT SWAIN PEABODY (1845–1917) was a product of the French educational system, but his knowledge of European and British architecture actually engendered in him a respect for early American architecture. Peabody was born in New Bedford, Massachusetts to the Reverend Dr. Ephraim Peabody and his wife Mary Jane Derby, who came from the prominent Salem, Massachusetts family of that name. Robert Peabody gained his undergraduate degree from Harvard College in 1866 and trained in the Boston architectural offices of Gridley J. F. Bryant and Henry Van Brunt. Not long after his graduation, he traveled to London and then to Paris, where he was a student at the Atelier Daumet, associated with the French state-supported art and architecture school of the Ecole des Beaux-arts. When Peabody returned to Boston in 1870, he formed an architectural partnership with John Goddard Stearns, Jr. (1843–1917), although he remained the principal designer.[1] Stearns was born and educated in New York City and studied engineering from 1861 at the Lawrence Scientific School at Harvard. Between 1863 and 1870 he worked for the architectural firm of Ware and Van Brunt, eventually becoming a draftsman. As a partner in Peabody & Stearns he bore responsibility for construction and field supervision.[2]

The architectural cultures Peabody experienced in England and France both were important to his thinking as he formulated a revival architecture specific to the United States, and to New England in particular. His education at the Ecole des Beaux-arts was significant in two respects. First, its pedagogy was based on the belief that the classical tradition supplied a set of forms that retained their validity as models through time. Although this idea was challenged from various quarters beginning in the 1820s and continuing through 1863, classical architecture remained a cornerstone of the school's teaching and of the student projects produced in the studios, or ateliers, affiliated with it.[3] (Two of Peabody's colleagues in Paris—Francis W. Chandler and Charles Follen McKim—would also become important historicist architects, in Boston and New York, respectively.) Second, drawing was of supreme importance at the Ecole des Beaux-arts. The most important drawing projects were the yearly competitions by which students advanced in the Ecole hierarchy, culminating in the Rome Prize competition, which provided its winners with a stint as government-supported fellows at the French Academy in Rome. Peabody described his participation in an 1868 competition thus:

> The examination was pretty hard, exciting, and as it was extended over a couple of weeks, worrisome and I was glad to have it over with ... For three consecutive days we went for 6 hours each day into an amphitheater and did our best at drawing from a difficult head of a caryatide [sic] that was put before us as a model. On the fourth day we were admitted at nine o'clock into a long room ... There we stayed twelve hours and I never did more work in three ordinary days I think.[4]

Peabody absorbed the Ecole's emphasis on drawing and passed it on to his drafts-men; he reportedly exhorted them to "Sketch! Sketch! And if you can't find any-thing else to sketch, sketch your boots!"[5]

Peabody's design method was also fundamentally indebted to his education at the Ecole des Beaux-arts; he once reflected that "Probably we all agree that the most interesting work which the profession has to offer—its highest refinement—is centered in the act of composition, of gathering and combining under the influence of imagination, or, if you please, of inspiration."[6] The Ecole placed great emphasis on composition, on the arrangement of the parts of a building in response to the parti, which constituted the guiding and unifying response to the program.

While Peabody's method as an architect grew from his experience in Paris, it was his travels through England that inspired him to promote the revival of early American architecture. Here he saw nineteenth-century buildings whose design was inspired by eighteenth-century (and earlier) architecture. In his talks and publications from the 1870s, Peabody showed how this style, the British Queen Anne movement, could serve as a model for American designers to develop a specifically and self-consciously American architecture. Just as their British con-temporaries had revived the forms associated with premodern buildings in Great Britain, Americans could similarly learn from surviving colonial- and federal-period buildings on this side of the Atlantic. He encouraged this point of view among the numerous draftsmen he and Stearns employed at their firm, many of

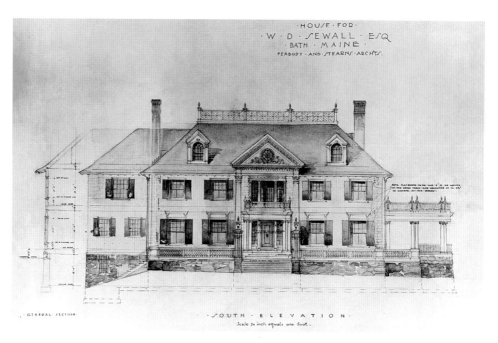

·HOUSE·FOR·
·W·D·SEWALL·ESQ
·BATH·MAINE·
PEABODY·AND·STEARNS·ARCHTS.

·GENERAL SECTION·   ·SOUTH·ELEVATION·
Scale ¼ inch equals one foot.

Peabody & Stearns, York Hall, the William D. Sewall House, Bath, 1896–98, elevation drawing

whom were familiar with historic architecture in northern New England and else-where. Having developed their revivalist aesthetic under Peabody's tutelage, these draftsmen (Arthur Little, for instance) went on to practice independently in a colonial revival idiom.

Peabody had a longstanding association with Maine, designing cottages on Islesboro and in the Mt. Desert Island communities of Bar Harbor, Northeast Harbor, and Seal Harbor. Many of these buildings incorporated neoclassical and other historicizing details into shingle-style designs. The Northeast Harbor cottage Peabody designed for Harvard president Charles Eliot, who had married Peabody's younger sister Ellen in 1858, is a case in point. The west elevation of the shingled and clapboarded house terminates in a lean-to roof, reminiscent of seventeenth-century buildings, while a Palladian window is incorporated into the north facade.[7]

—K.D.M.

York Hall, the William D. Sewall House, 1896–98
Bath

BUILT TWO DECADES after Robert Peabody's initial call for American architects to follow the lead of English Queen Anne designers by reviving earlier buildings in their new works, York Hall clearly represents the historicist aesthetic Peabody had advocated. By the time the house was constructed, Peabody's pioneering appeal for the emulation of early American architecture in new building had achieved the status of dogma among many designers in the Northeast.

Bath is less important as a resort than as a shipbuilding center on the Kennebec River and is the site today of the Bath Iron Works. York Hall was originally built here for William D. Sewall, who was a member of an important shipbuilding family that had successfully made the transition from wooden- to steel-hull construction.

York Hall, facade

William's son Sumner Sewall, who went on to serve as Maine's governor between 1941 and 1945, is said to have been christened on August 5, 1897, the same day that the house was christened York Hall, in honor of the Sewalls' historic roots in York, Maine. The neoclassical architecture of the family residence recalls the mansions of earlier generations of prosperous shipbuilders and owners.

The hip roof, five-bay facade, and classicizing details of York Hall all tie it visually to the federal-period architecture of coastal Maine. Exquisitely preserved, the house effectively illustrates the revival of the earlier merchant aesthetic at the turn of the century. As a contemporary description of York Hall suggests, Peabody successfully conveyed his historic sources as well as a sense of expansiveness that underscored the Sewall family's local importance:

> Passing through the doorway one enters a spacious reception hall, with a broad, winding stairway on the farther end. On the left is the dining room, on the right, the drawing room. Adjoining the latter apartment is the library, in the northeastern corner. These rooms, with the reception hall are included in the main apartments on the street floor. Each has richly tiled fireplaces with mantel spaces very high and strictly colonial. Broad, sliding doors when open, will make the lower floor seem like a palace ballroom.[8]

Although the house had a historical character, it was clearly planned to meet the functional requirements of its turn-of-the-century inhabitants. Given that Sewall family members were leaders in the local shipbuilding industry and also politically active, it is not surprising that Peabody designed York Hall to easily accommodate large gatherings of people. If throughout his career the architect was a passionate advocate of historic New England architecture, he nevertheless recognized the need to adjust his prototypes to modern uses.

—K.D.M.

York Hall, dining room

York Hall, stair hall

York Hall, china cabinet

The Bangor Public Library, 1911–14
Bangor

DESIGNED NEAR THE end of Robert Peabody's life, the Bangor Public Library illustrates his ongoing commitment to neoclassical design. While Peabody explicitly
referred to local architecture in other Maine commissions, such as York Hall in
Bath, the public function of a library necessitated a less domestic and more monumental neoclassical idiom. Indeed, the Bangor Public Library possesses many of the
architectural elements that had denoted public functions and significance since the
time of ancient Rome. The central dome, for example, emphasizes the main
entrance in the symmetrical facade. And the library is constructed of masonry—
reserved since the eighteenth century largely for public buildings in northern
Maine—as opposed to the less durable wood-frame construction common in residential buildings. Its use adds a sense of permanence and grandeur to the library.

Peabody & Stearns,
the Bangor Public Library,
Bangor, 1911–14, facade

Peabody & Stearns won the competition to design the Bangor Public Library over several other firms that had been invited to participate. The library's architectural advisor for the competition, Francis W. Chandler, had been a fellow draftsman with Peabody at the Boston firm of Ware and Van Brunt, and Chandler and Peabody had become friends for life. The latter was chosen over Maine architects including the well-known Bar Harbor designer of cottages and other buildings, Frederick L. Savage, and the Boston firm of McLean and Wright.[9]

The Bangor Public Library

At the time of its construction, the Bangor Public Library was heralded as "by far [the] finest in Maine."[10] The opulence of the interior appointments—and especially of the main stair hall, which was lit by "[a] double dome of glass and steel, from which is to be suspended a massive and ornate chandelier containing white opal candles"—caught the eye of contemporary observers.[11] Also worthy of note were twelve tablets "embellished with a wealth of decorative detail and inscribed to famous men of letters" encircling the base of the dome.[12] These literary figures included Henry Wadsworth Longfellow, Francis Parkman, and Ralph Waldo Emerson, among others. Thus, while the classically derived architecture connected the library with the very foundations of Western culture, the authors memorialized under the dome linked the building to the New England literary tradition.

The interior layout of the Bangor Public Library conformed to an arrangement that was common for such buildings at the turn of the twentieth century. The domed space at the center contained the circulation desk as well as the stairway to second-story meeting and lecture rooms. To either side were located reading rooms with fireplaces. Above these rooms, on the upper floors, were the book stacks. The building has been subsequently expanded to serve its continued function as a library.

The library is an impressive example of how Peabody adapted the classical tradition to contemporary functional requirements; it is also one of two public commissions, along with the nearby Bangor High School of approximately the same period, that reestablished the city's commercial and cultural importance following a major fire on April 30, 1911.[13]

—K.D.M.

Francis W. Chandler

A SECOND ARCHITECTURE office that became an important center for the colonial revival was headed by Francis Ward Chandler (1844–1926). He was born in Boston and attended the Lancaster Academy as well as Harvard College, where he was a student in 1861, at the beginning of the Civil War. Chandler served for two years, then became a student draftsman for the Boston firm of Ware and Van Brunt, well known for their Neogothic designs. It was here that he met Robert Peabody, who was to become his close friend. The two traveled to Paris together in 1867, becoming students at the Atelier Daumet, which was associated with the Ecole des Beaux-arts.

After returning from Paris in 1869, Chandler assisted Professor William R. Ware, the founder of the school of architecture at the Massachusetts Institute of Technology. In 1871 he became assistant to the supervising architect for the U.S. Treasury Department in Philadelphia. At that time Chandler also founded a short-lived architectural firm with his cousin, Theophilus Chandler, which was disbanded in October 1871. When he returned to Boston four years later, Chandler formed a partnership with Edward Clark Cabot (1818–1901), the architect of the Italianate Boston Athenaeum (1847) and the first president of the Boston Society of Architects, from 1867 to 1896. Under Cabot's presidency, the society provided a forum for the discussion of earlier American architecture. Among other events, the group organized an exhibition of drawings by architect Charles Bulfinch in 1878 and a lecture on the historic buildings of Philadelphia (held by Robert Peabody) and the Jamaica Plain neighborhood of Boston. Cabot himself spoke to the group on the historic houses of North Carolina.[14]

Before the partnership with Chandler was established, Cabot had already become involved in the development of the new Back Bay neighborhood of Boston as a row house architect.[15] The designs Cabot later produced with his architectural partner showed a change of aesthetic direction away from the Italianate idiom he had used when working independently. Together, Cabot and Chandler produced a number of Back Bay row house designs that represent their interest in the Queen Anne movement. The facades of houses at 178 Marlborough Street (1879) and 135

Marlborough Street (1880), for example, both incorporate pressed and cut brick decoration, which was used extensively in Queen Anne architecture; the particular motifs employed—sunflowers, for instance—were also favorites of contemporary British architects.[16]

In 1888 Chandler became the head of the architecture program at MIT.[17] At a banquet on the occasion of Chandler's retirement from the MIT faculty in 1912, William Barry recalled of his time as a draftsman with the firm: "It was the human element we loved in the place.... There was a good deal of New England spirit in the office which Mr. Chandler ran."[18] That "spirit" likely referred to the generosity of the older generation of men who mentored the young draftsmen. It probably also meant, for Barry, appreciating the region's architectural heritage and putting it at the center of a new revival style.

—K.D.M.

Francis W. Chandler, the Paralyso, North Haven, 1884–85

The Paralyso, 1884–85
North Haven

The Paralyso, 1884–85,
with later additions and
alterations

OF THE APPROXIMATELY three thousand islands off the coast of Maine, a few became favored as summer resorts for urbanites by the end of the nineteenth century. Among them was the island of North Haven, located some twelve miles off Rockland, Maine, with an unspoiled landscape and only a modest collection of buildings. Through the nineteenth century, the island adjacent to North Haven,

Vinalhaven, became one of the most important centers for the quarrying of granite on the Maine coast, supplying the material for the Brooklyn Bridge and other well-known urban structures.[19] As late as the 1880s, North Haven, however, had witnessed little commercial or industrial development, making it attractive to the Bostonians who "discovered" the island as a summer resort.

The island already had a year-round community sustained by fishing and farming, but the arrival of summer residents increased economic activity and created a need for additional housing, particularly seasonal cottages. The first building Francis W. Chandler designed for North Haven was the Paralyso, whose name was derived from its original function. The Paralyso served as a kind of clubhouse for the Boston men (Chandler among them) who built it and formed the nucleus of the summer community. There they drank and smoked, perhaps becoming "paralyzed." Later the Paralyso was adapted to its current function as a summer cottage.

Chandler's design for the building played off of the local vernacular rather than imposing a foreign architectural vocabulary on the place. As North Haven historian Roger Reed has pointed out, "Chandler designed a structure that in materials, scale, and configuration conformed to the vernacular buildings in North Haven's harbor." The Paralyso sits practically in the water, supported by granite piers that barely raise it beyond the swells. While the building has few elaborate historical details—or none, for that matter—its overall form is suggestive of earlier architecture. Its original rear lean-to, or saltbox, roof profile in particular connects it to eighteenth-century houses.[20]

By the time that the Paralyso was constructed, appreciation of Maine's vernacular architecture was beginning to become widespread. Maine novelist Sarah Orne Jewett, for instance, wrote of the state's Queen Anne–style pavilion at the 1893 World's Columbian Exposition in Chicago:

> The Maine building may be a well-planned building, but it does not speak for Maine. It ought to have been a great, square house, with a hip roof and dormer windows, and a railing round the chimneys. The best houses in all our best Maine towns were built so a hundred years ago, and nothing looks so well in our Maine landscape, or in the pleasant streets of our villages.[21]

Jewett's point regarding the appropriate model for contemporary architecture is well taken and recalls Chandler's efforts on North Haven: the architect would certainly have agreed with Jewett's argument that federal-period architecture is well-adapted to Maine's landscape and can inspire new building.

—K.D.M.

The Palace, 1887
Addition, 1916
North Haven

Francis W. Chandler, the Palace, North Haven, 1887 (above), and with addition, 1916 (right)

CHANDLER'S FIRST TRIP to North Haven was made by boat and with the woman whom he would later marry, Alice Daland. As the architect's family expanded—his wife bore him two children in the mid to late 1890s—he continued to spend time on the island and designed the Palace as his family's summer cottage. His design

58

for the cottage (just as his earlier North Haven building, the Paralyso) respected local architectural tradition and is a testament to Chandler's commitment to using historic architecture as a building model. As Roger Reed has pointed out, the house, with its clapboards and avoidance of any elaborate details, conforms to local expectations for residential buildings.[22] It is its siting alone that sets the cottage apart from the year-round houses on North Haven. Seated on a rise overlooking the water and built with a porch that emerges from an outcropping of rock, the Palace was situated to take advantage of the view as well as the cool breezes off Penobscot Bay. Those were preeminently the concerns of summer visitors but had been relatively less important in shaping the construction of houses for the small local community.

The open porch, or "verandah," was the feature sine qua non of the nineteenth-century cottage. In the 1932 novel *Mary's Neck*, in which he fictionalized the summer community at Kennebunkport, Indiana writer Booth Tarkington underscores the importance of the verandah and goes so far as to suggest that its size was an index of a summer resident's wealth. As narrator he describes a meeting with a venerable resident of Mary's Neck, one Mr. Massey, who "drove over to Cobble Neck to see me and express himself in a long talk on my modest but breezy verandah." Later, the narrator returns the visit: "I went to Mary's Neck, and, without much inquiry found [Mr. Massey's] cottage, for it was the largest on the crest of the coastal rocks and of itself rather conspicuous evidence of Mr. Massey's worldly prosperity. He was in a long wicker chair upon his verandah."[23]

In 1897 Chandler designed a third North Haven cottage, the Anchorage, which was larger than the earlier cottages but in keeping with them stylistically. In addition to this handful of cottages, Chandler also produced two designs for model lifesaving stations, in 1873 and 1875. Six U.S. Lifesaving Stations in Maine have been identified as having been based on Chandler's design. Although he did not build any other cottages in Maine, Chandler nonetheless continued to have a personal connection with the state, spending summers on North Haven until the time of his death.[24]

—K.D.M.

William Ralph Emerson

WILLIAM RALPH EMERSON (1833–1917) established an architectural firm in Boston in which appreciation of New England's architectural heritage flourished. He emphasized the importance of recording earlier architecture—by encouraging his draftsmen to draw—and argued for the use of eighteenth- and early nineteenth-century buildings as models for new designs.

Emerson, born in Illinois, had roots in Maine through his parents, Olive Bourne and Dr. William S. Emerson, who were originally from Kennebunk. When the elder William Emerson died in 1837, his wife and children returned to Kennebunk, although they also spent some time with a Boston relative. In 1854 William Ralph Emerson started training as an architect with Jonathan Preston (1801–1888) in Boston and became his partner several years later. During the period in which he promoted colonial architecture among his draftsmen—the 1860s and early 1870s—he had various professional relationships: Emerson worked on his own in the early 1860s and had a firm with Carl Fehmer (1838–circa 1916) for about a decade beginning in 1864. After that time he practiced independently once more.

Old Ship Meetinghouse, Hingham, Mass., 1681, with additions from 1731 and 1755, and restorations from the late 1860s and 1930

As a partner in Emerson & Fehmer he evidently had an important role in the firm's commissions in the recently developed Back Bay section of Boston and elsewhere. Although this phase of Emerson's career is poorly documented, it seems that it was during this time that his interest in early American architecture first developed. On May 21, 1869 he gave a talk on the significance of colonial architecture in New England to the Boston Society of Architects. At this point he was involved in the restoration of the Old Ship Church in Hingham, a seventeenth-century meetinghouse that had been extensively altered in the eighteenth century.[25] More fashionable neoclassical details had been added during the earlier restoration as well as a ceiling (later removed) that masked the massive timber frame, which was frequently likened to the hull of a ship. Emerson's work was later criticized as part of a series of nineteenth-century alterations, made mostly "to the detriment of the building."[26] However, he actually appears to have acted judiciously, preserving much of the eighteenth-century work and inserting leaded-glass, diamond-paned windows into pilastered frames in the hope to "recall the spirit of the seventeenth century," as a later critic wrote, "but which, unfortunately, are neither one thing nor the other."[27] This criticism notwithstanding, it is interesting that at this relatively early stage in the history of architectural restoration in the United States, Emerson was taking such a careful approach to the significant additions that had been made to the building after its original construction. Emerson's work on the Old Ship Church demonstrated respect both for the massively framed seventeenth-century structure and the neoclassical alterations that had been made later.

His wide-ranging architectural interests are also evident in Emerson's designs for new buildings. He is among a handful of architects, including Frederick L. Savage, John Calvin Stevens, and H. H. Richardson, credited with having popularized the shingle style for domestic buildings in New England, especially in the region's newly developed suburbs and resorts. His style blended historicist elements drawn from English Queen Anne architecture—such as halftimbering, small-paned windows, and cluster chimneys—with forms borrowed from earlier American buildings. His cottages were clad largely in wood shingles and often included features—delicately detailed balustrades and Palladian windows, for example—based on early classically derived buildings in the United States.

Emerson clearly favored the British neoclassical tradition that had been passed on to New England architects and builders around the turn of the nineteenth century. In 1889 he wrote that

> It is fortunate that the old New England builders never had a French training, but were brought up on the old "Builder's Guides," and did [so] before Caesar [sic] Daly had flooded the literature of the art with voluminous unhealthiness, and that Charles Bulfinch studied the works of Sir Christopher Wrenn [sic] and Sir William Chambers and ignored the French masters altogether.[28]

In early American architecture, Emerson found a methodical approach to design, which contrasted with what he perceived as the unreasonable excesses of the architecture of his own time. Emerson imparted his appreciation for classical restraint to his students, draftsmen, and friends, including John Calvin Stevens and William E. Barry, who would become important architects of the colonial revival movement.

—K.D.M.

Charles P. Clark House, *or* Capt. Nathaniel Lord House, 1898
Kennebunkport

IN RENOVATING THE Captain Nathaniel Lord House for its turn-of-the-century owner Charles P. Clark, president of the New York and New Haven Railroad, William Ralph Emerson exhibited a deeply respectful attitude toward what he referred to on the plans as the "old house."[29] Indeed, by the time that Emerson came to expand the house, it was already recognized as an important Kennebunkport landmark. Its iconic status is celebrated in a painting from around 1920 by Willard Leroy Metcalf (1858–1925). The painter's sunny view of the Lord House recalls architect Frank Wallis's description of a common romantic attraction to early American neoclassicism:

> I venture to say that most of you . . . have, at some time or other, dreamed of retiring for your mellow dotage to some old white clapboarded house, set a little back from the street, with elms shading the front. . . . Hollyhocks, petunias, verbenas and old-fashioned pinks border the herring-bone brick walk up to the portico—a pediment portico or one with upper balcony, it matters little. You insist, however, on having

William Ralph Emerson, addition to the Charles P. Clark House, or Capt. Nathaniel Lord House, Kennebunkport, 1898

63

the fluted Doric or Corinthian columns, with flat pilasters against the wall framing the arched doorway—an elliptic arch, please, with radiating divisions in iron and little lead roses at the intersection.[30]

The appeal of the Lord House for Clark may have had something to do with such nostalgia for its classically derived forms, framed by graceful elms and old-fashioned plantings, while its notoriety may have been due, in part, to William Barry's interest in the building. He recorded many of the houses built by Thomas Eaton—the William Lord House, the Taylor-Barry House, Wallingford Hall, and the First Parish Church in Kennebunk among them, as well as this house, built for Nathaniel Lord in 1814. During the late 1860s or early 1870s, Barry produced pen-and-ink drawings of the Lord House, some with watercolor wash, and published a perspective view in his book *Pen Sketches of Old Houses* (1874).

The Charles P. Clark House, from *Pen Sketches of Old Houses* (1874)

Emerson's client, Charles P. Clark, must have been a man of substantial means as the head of a large and profitable corporation. Chartered in 1872, the New York and New Haven Railroad expanded through the end of the century, absorbing a number of smaller lines. In 1890 the company's revenue was more than one hundred million dollars; it employed four thousand people and served twelve million passengers each year. The renovation of the Lord House was undertaken at the height of the company's prosperity.[31]

Instead of building an expansive cottage at Cape Arundel, as other wealthy summer residents had done, Clark decided to hire a summer-cottage architect—Emerson—to add the most desirable features of a modern house to the historic building and to expand it to meet the needs of a wealthy owner and his household staff. The new three-story wing replaced an altered rear extension and contained back stairs for the use of the servants, a modern kitchen, and a servant's dining room. An existing kitchen with a large hearth with bake oven was transformed into a new dining room. The wide fireplace was complemented by the beamed ceiling that Emerson introduced—together these features produced an appropriately "colonial" atmosphere.

Adapting an earlier kitchen to serve as a dining room or sitting room became commonplace for architects renovating period houses at the turn of the

Willard Leroy Metcalf, "Captain Lord House, Kennebunkport," oil on canvas, circa 1920, the Florence Griswold Museum

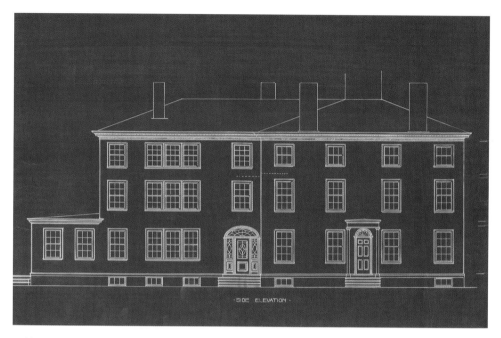

Addition to the Charles P. Clark House, elevation

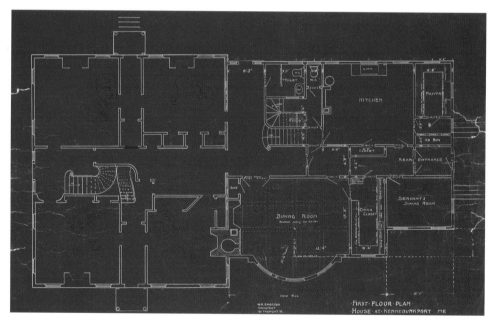

Addition to the Charles P. Clark House, first-floor plan

century and later. As popular architecture writers Harold Donaldson Eberlein and Donald Greene Tarpley commented in 1933:

> What was the kitchen before may become in a new scheme a living-room or a dining-room and prove infinitely more satisfactory in its new capacity. In many an old farmhouse, the most important room was the kitchen with its ample space for the general household occupations, and its large fireplace equipped with a crane, where all the cooking was done. In the remodeling scheme, this room will oftentimes offer every ideal requirement for a living-room in respect of exposure, size, shape, and place in plan, while the kitchen might quite as well, or probably better, be in some other room, or, perhaps, in a new addition where all the modern appointments could be installed at less cost and with less inconvenience.[32]

Although the Nathaniel Lord House could hardly be considered an "old farmhouse," its renovation by Emerson nonetheless conformed to the pattern described by Eberlein and Tarpley. Made obsolete by late nineteenth-century household technologies, the hearth in the former kitchen became a powerful symbol of the historic character of the building.

The choice of Emerson to undertake the transformation of the Lord House was fortuitous. Not only did he have a personal connection to the Kennebunks, but since the 1860s, he had been a vocal advocate for early American architecture; in his May 1869 "sermon" to the Boston Society of Architects, he railed against the "destruction of old New England houses," which he pronounced the only true American architecture that had yet existed.[33] In accordance with his beliefs, Emerson judiciously stepped his addition back from the sides of the old house so that it would not overwhelm the historic front block. He also echoed the neoclassical aspects of Eaton's design in the bay with a modest balustrade that he incorporated into the new dining room.[34] ❀

—K.D.M.

The Draftsmen

William E. Barry

The Taylor-Barry House
The Colonel Frederick H. Harris Cottage
The Robertson House
The Parsons Beach Commissions
Thornton Academy Library
Thornton Academy Headmaster's House

John Calvin Stevens

The Cape Arundel Commissions
York Institute

Henry Paston Clark

The Kennebunkport Commissions

Arthur Little, OF LITTLE & BROWNE

Hamilton House

Mary Sowles Perkins and Elizabeth Bishop Perkins

The Elizabeth Perkins House

William H. Dabney, OF BALL & DABNEY

The Sorrento Public Library
The Stadpole Block

Thomas Eaton, Wallingford Hall, Kennebunk, 1804–06

William E. Barry

THE RELATIONSHIP BETWEEN Robert Peabody and his draftsmen seems to have been mutually advantageous: He taught them about architectural practice, and they contributed in important ways to the firm's designs. William E. Barry (1846–1932), for example, is thought to have helped with the designs of the Nathan Matthews House (1871–72) in Newport, Rhode Island and Pierre Lorillard's cottage, The Breakers (1877–78), also at Newport. The Breakers incorporated certain colonial motifs suggesting that the firm was beginning to emerge as a center for the investigation of earlier American architecture. The house also possesses the irregular massing, cluster chimneys, and other details associated with the British Queen Anne style, underscoring Peabody's reliance on contemporary English architecture in developing an American revival style.

William E. Barry, Wallingford Hall, from *Pen Sketches of Old Houses* (1874)

That Barry shared Peabody's admiration for earlier neoclassicism is hardly surprising, given his background. From early childhood on he had shown a facility for drawing and a fascination for architecture (evident in some of his childhood works in the Barry Collection at the Brick Store Museum in Kennebunk, Maine) and, after his early education at local schools in Kennebunk, he pursued training as an architect. He began his apprenticeship in the office of William Ralph Emerson, with whom he was distantly related, in Boston in the spring of 1864. As Barry reported to his mother, he immediately began a course of study under the architect's direction:

> I like Mr. Emerson, also, he is first rate, you ought to hear him talk. He gave me
> something to draw, (copy) & c...He shew me several sketches that he had made,

William E. Barry, French
Second Empire Residence,
pen and ink drawing with
watercolor wash, circa 1867

finely done, & with sepia I believe, I shall learn in due time. He has given me several
books to look over on perspective & c.[1]

The education that Barry received from Emerson was supplemented by courses he
took at the Lowell Institute. He learned mainly on the job, however, reporting in
November 1864, that he had been "busy lately on the plans for a house at
Weymouth [Massachusetts]. I have regular work now. Do not originate of course,
but copy plans & such things which are to be used & sent away."[2] A group of Barry's
drawings dating to this period includes elevations of French Second Empire residences, a neoclassical church, and details of an Eastlake-style building, all carefully
shaded with watercolor wash.

Barry left Emerson's office in 1866 and soon thereafter joined the firm of
Martin and Thayer as a draftsman, but the firm disbanded in 1867. Drawings of two
garrison houses in York, Maine date from that year, showing that Barry was already
deeply involved in documenting the historic architecture of southern Maine.[3]
Returning to Boston in 1869, Barry went to work for the firm of Hartwell and
Swasey, where he remained, with interruptions for travel to the American South,
until he joined the Boston firm of Peabody & Stearns. By the time that Barry joined
that fledgling office, he was already experienced in working with historic American
neoclassical architecture, and was well versed in contemporary British and conti-
nental European developments. Barry did not only contribute to the designs of
Peabody's early colonial revival houses, but has also been credited with having
assisted his fellow draftsman at Peabody & Stearns, Arthur Little, with his first independent commission, a house called Cliffs at Manchester, Massachusetts in 1879.

Barry was just as interested in the history of the pre-industrial period as he was
in its architecture. He erected a number of historic markers around York County,
Maine and authored several historical studies, including *Sketch of an Old River* (1888),
A Stroll by a Familiar River (1909), *Chronicles of Kennebunk* (1923), *A Stroll Thro' the
Past* (1933), and others.[4] Many of these works focused on the period when Kennebunk
and Kennebunkport had been important shipping and shipbuilding centers, from
just after the Revolution up to the advent of steamships and larger-hulled vessels. By
1872 the construction of wooden ships in the Kennebunks was already something of

an exception; Barry wrote to his grandfather William Lord in the summer of that year that he was "glad to hear that there is a prospect of ship building at the Port," implying that shipbuilding was in decline. Barry expresses, in the same letter, the hope that "no more railroads will go near Kennebunk."[5] He seems to have been uncomfortable with the change he saw taking place around him, and less ambitious to advance his professional position than to immerse himself in the history and architecture of the early Republic, when his forebears had been socially, politically, and economically dominant in southern Maine. By the 1870s brick mills had appeared in Kennebunk and virtually dominated the landscapes of the cities of Biddeford and Saco just to the north. For Barry then, embracing earlier architecture may have been partly motivated by his resistance to modernization and the change it entailed.

At the time of Barry's death in 1932, his heirs discovered in his house "that upstairs, his boyhood bedroom was used for his workroom. Here, on an architect's drafting table, he labored over plans for local buildings, seashore cottages and did his writing and drawing. We found clippings, notes on scraps of paper, sketches, prints and plans everywhere."[6] Unfortunately, only a small portion of that material was preserved, and knowledge of many of Barry's local commissions was lost after his death.[7] It is clear, however, that after his return to Kennebunk with his wife, Florence Wallingford Hooper, in 1883, he operated an active local architectural practice. The Barrys moved into what had

The Cliff House, Kennebunkport, 1881, expansion and renovation by William E. Barry, 1906, postcard, circa 1910

been his wife's family home, the federal-period Wallingford Hall, which Barry had drawn earlier. From here he designed buildings that served the summer community as well as the growing year-round town of Kennebunk.[8] Like many of the other architects who began their careers in the offices of Boston architects William Ralph Emerson, Robert Peabody, and Francis Chandler, William Barry devoted a substantial proportion of his time to designing cottages for middle-class and wealthier summer residents of coastal Maine. He also served the local population by designing churches, libraries, and buildings for other essential institutions in Kennebunk and surrounding towns.

—K.D.M.

Thomas Eaton, the Taylor-Barry House, Kennebunk, circa 1803–04, with additions and alterations by William E. Barry, 1871–74

The Taylor-Barry House

Originally built by Thomas Eaton, circa 1803–04
With additions and alterations by William E. Barry, 1871–74
Kennebunk

IN *HISTORIC HOMES OF EARLY AMERICA* (1927) Elise Lathrop describes visiting some of Kennebunk's fine neoclassical houses. In her words,

> The Taylor-Barry House is another fine example of those built by well-to-do Maine sea captains, in the palmy days of our merchant marine. In the spacious rooms on both floors are beautiful woodwork and mantels.... This house is wonderfully well built, with twelve-foot ceilings, two-foot underpinnings, two feet high, and with an eighth-inch thick brick wall with an airspace between it and the outer walls of wood, thus insuring against the bitter cold of winter. It has a beautiful winding staircase with two landings, the rail of mahogany. Retired sea captains usually had mahogany trim in the fine houses which they built for themselves along the New England coast, and it is in seaport towns, as a rule, that the handsomest old houses are found in New England.[9]

William E. Barry, the Taylor-Barry House, pen and ink drawing with watercolor wash, circa 1870

WINDOW SEAT IN HALL

William E. Barry, the Taylor-Barry House, window, from *Pen Sketches of Old Houses* (1874)

William Barry evidently shared Lathrop's esteem for the Taylor-Barry House, since he began recording it in perspective views with watercolor wash as early as the 1860s. Like Lathrop he admired the composition ornament on the fireplace mantels—the use of which Thomas Eaton pioneered—drawing those motifs and publishing them in his *Pen Sketches of Old Houses* (1874). By that date, his mother, Sarah Cleaves Lord Barry Perkins, had already purchased the house from her cousin Claudius Buchanan Williams, a master mariner, who had bought the mansion from his father's estate for the sum of $4,550 on January 17, 1862. The house had been in the Williams family for decades.

The renovation of his mother's house was Barry's first independent commission. Sarah Perkins and her second husband, Jott Stone Perkins, a ship's captain, began renovations to the building in 1871, which continued through 1874, despite Jott Perkins's death in November of 1871. Their first alteration was the construction of a piazza, designed by Barry, along the east side to replace a paneled brick terrace. The piazza would have provided an outdoor space with optimal southern and eastern exposure in a location protected by the house's ell, shed, and barn to the north. In August 1871 William wrote to his mother that "the piazza is...near completed by this time. Am glad of the improvement but will not forget the brick terrace as long as memory lasts."[10] Such attachment to the original features of the house was a sentiment that Sarah and William shared. In 1872 Barry designed a portico for the Summer Street (south) entrance, which was completed in spring 1873. Barry described the portico as having "four pillars in front, two against the house, a pediment in front and chains on the side in imitation of the old style."[11]

Although Barry and his mother were not above dressing up the rather plain exterior of the four-square house, adding with the portico and piazza some of the common features of a middle-class house of the late nineteenth century, they viewed the original portions of the interior as sacrosanct. By the time that Sarah Perkins bought the house, in May 1871, it had already been substantially altered on the interior by the previous owner, Williams. The most important change attributed to Williams was the replacement of moldings and fireplace surrounds in the east front rooms of the house. In an apparent effort to make at least part of the house more fashionable, larger ceiling moldings with more boldly scaled components were installed in the dining room and the chamber above it. Carved marble mantel-pieces were also installed in the chimney breasts on that side. The Perkinses had the interior painted and wallpapered,[12] but they seem to have mostly refrained from continuing the updating begun by Williams. In a letter written to her son around May 1871, Sarah indicated her intention to preserve the original federal-period character of the house, stating, "That old fashioned parlor, I shall not have touched, to make any changes, the house is in good repair."[13]

The Taylor-Barry House, parlor fireplace detail, from *Pen Sketches of Old Houses* (1874)

Although neither William nor his brother Charles was living in their parents' house at the time they took up residence on Summer Street, each had a room designated for his use in the Taylor-Barry House. As Sarah wrote to William at the time of the purchase, "I have appropriated the back corner [northwest] chamber next to Grandfather's for you, and the opposite one for Charley, and I shall take the front southern chamber." On April 9, 1873 William wrote to his brother that "[I] have renovated the small entry room next [to] mine [and] taken the glass off the bureau and have father's writing desk there all prepared to receive papers, where I shall collect all that are of value."[14] Barry's description of the work that would go on in the room is revealing: already he was sifting through family papers and organizing them into an archive that would eventually become the core of the Brick Store Museum's collection, which his niece Edith Barry founded in 1936.

Upon Sarah Perkins's death in 1904, William Barry bought out his brother's interest in the Taylor-Barry House and became its sole owner. He occupied it with his wife, Florence Wallingford Barry, until her death in 1925 and continued living there alone until his own death in 1932. (Their children, Ernest Lord Barry and Helen Wallingford Barry, had died in 1886 and 1907, respectively.) William Barry seems to have made few, if any, changes to the Taylor-Barry House while he owned

The Taylor-Barry House, parlor

it, again, likely out of respect for its historic and architectural significance. His admiration of the building was so strong that he apparently resisted its modernization even late in his life when he refused to have the house electrified. Indeed, as early as 1871, Barry had expressed disregard for "modern" amenities in houses, declaring that "[I] am doing a city house [for the architectural firm of Peabody & Stearns] of which we build many. They are warm enough and have every convenience, bells, hot air, water pipes of every description. I would not live in such a house. I would take one of those old black affairs over in Kennebunkport any day in preference."[15]

The modernization of the house thus had to wait until it passed into the hands of the children of William's brother Charles in 1932. Charles Edward Barry, Julia Barry Bodman, and Edith Cleaves Barry owned the house together until 1949 when Charles and his wife Pat purchased a house at 35 Summer Street for their use. When Edith Barry died in 1969, the Brick Store Museum received her half-interest in the house. The remaining half became the museum's at Julia Bodman's death in 1971.

—K.D.M.

The Taylor-Barry House, portico addition

The Colonel Frederick H. Harris Cottage, 1893
Kennebunk Beach

THE HARRIS COTTAGE occupies a dramatic outcropping between Boothby's Beach and Pebble Beach, just north of Lord's Point. An existing cottage on the site, built in the early 1870s, was purchased by Colonel Frederick H. Harris of Montclair, New Jersey in 1888. In May 1892 the cottage burned and was replaced by this house, designed by Barry.[16] Although it was built about fifteen years after Barry's first efforts to blend the Queen Anne and colonial revival styles as a draftsman for Peabody & Stearns, the Harris Cottage still evidences a similar blend of design concepts.

The underlying mass of the house is of the familiar cross-gable type. Popular with Queen Anne architects, such houses consisted of two intersecting rectangular blocks with gabled roofs, offering more visual variety than a simpler rectangular block. The projecting gabled mass placed a plethora of details on the street side, and the intersection between the two parts of the house often occasioned a tower. Here, however, Barry creates visual richness while maintaining the restraint of the classical tradition, which he so admired. The basic plan type easily accommodates a verandah—essential for the oceanfront site—which wraps around the southwest end of the house, protected on the northern side by the cross-gable massing. The slender paired columns of this porch betray Barry's

William E. Barry, the Colonel Frederick Harris Cottage, Kennebunk Beach, 1893

81

The Colonel Frederick
Harris Cottage, facade

neoclassical leanings. Window hoods and cornice brackets are among the other elements that add texture to the exterior.

Perhaps the most interesting elevation faces the street. The entrance projects from the southeast corner of the house, while the center section of the facade, where the front door might be expected, features a series of arched windows that create a dramatic bay in the dining room. Elsewhere in the house—in the gables and dormers—the motif of the arched window, inspired by late eighteenth-century architecture, is repeated in various combinations, linking the facades to each other. Barry's evocation of earlier houses is also evident in the delicate balustrade above the front bay, which serves as a railing for a second-story porch. The transition between this projecting center bay and the north section of the street facade is made by the back door. Its small porch, with an openwork surround that echoes the balustrade of the center block, extends upward into a stairway enclosure. The shed roof of this stairway continues the roof line of the central block down to the first story. Together the two rooflines suggest a lean-to, or saltbox, profile of a seventeenth- or eighteenth-century New England house. Thus Barry layers over an essentially Queen Anne house details reminiscent of some of the earlier buildings he so admired.

The cross-gable massing resulted in a four-room plan on the first story, with the living and dining rooms connected by archways reminiscent of federal-period architecture. On the second story, the cross-gable massing gave each of the several bedrooms a spectacular ocean view. The interior walls were finished in unpainted wood, creating an informal atmosphere appropriate to a summer cottage. Barry clearly labored over the fireplaces, for which numerous preparatory sketches survive among his drawings at the Brick Store Museum. The mantelpieces typically feature a molded surround, inspired perhaps by historic houses in the area, and Queen Anne–style overmantels. They have elaborate scrollwork and shelves and would have been ideal for displaying the owners' collections of artistic objects or shells collected along the shore.

Colonel Harris and William Barry likely came in contact with one another through Barry's brother Charles, who, like Colonel Harris, lived in Montclair, New Jersey. Barry had also designed a number of other cottages in the immediate vicinity of the Harris house.[17]

—K.D.M.

The Robertson House, 1891
Kennebunkport

THE ROBERTSON HOUSE in Kennebunkport clearly demonstrates the link between Barry's recording of historic architecture in his drawings and the subsequent use of those models in his architectural practice. More specifically, the design shows Barry incorporating aspects of his grandfather's, William Lord's, house in Kennebunk, into a work of his own. The house was built by Charles C. Perkins as a wedding gift for his daughter Evaline Perkins Titcomb Robertson. Reportedly, it did not suit Mrs. Robertson's idea of an appropriate summer residence, however, for she subsequently sold it and built a much larger summer house nearby.[18]

Although the Robertson House may not have corresponded to the client's concept of a summer cottage, it did fit nicely into its surroundings, located as it was on a street lined with early American buildings. In its design Barry assimilated neoclassical details to a common nineteenth-century house type. Essentially it is a four-square house, its two stories differentiated in the perspective drawing by the use of clapboards below and shingles above. The bay window on the side of the house was a popular feature of domestic design beginning in the mid-nineteenth century. Onto this common two-story massing, Barry layered details extrapolated from his grandfather's house, which he had pictured earlier in his *Pen Sketches of Old Houses*. The most striking relationship to the William Lord mansion is the handling of the roof. While the hip roof of the Robertson House is steeper than that of the Lord mansion, it has a similar gabled monitor. On the Lord mansion, this monitor runs from front to rear, while

William E. Barry, the Robertson House, Kennebunkport, 1891, perspective drawing

on the Robertson House it is parallel to the front wall of the building. On the interior, the Robertson House follows a basically Georgian plan, although it is adapted to nineteenth-century expectations for residential architecture. The center hall, for example—a salient feature of the Georgian type—was widened by Barry to give it the feel of a "living hall" as popularized by Norman Shaw and his followers.

Barry seems to have appreciated Kennebunkport as a quiet village whose imposing dignity came from its collection of older houses. His design for the Robertson House, built at time when many in-town houses sprouted all manner of late-Victorian exuberances such as towers and various shaped dormers, instead was modeled on perhaps the most staid of the historic styles that had enjoyed local popularity. Barry's view of Kennebunkport was akin to that expressed later by author and local summer resident Booth Tarkington in his 1930 novel *Mirthful Haven*. Describing a fictionalized Kennebunkport, Tarkington wrote:

> Away from the tumbled coast and the rocky woodland of pine and juniper, the village itself, like some outpost wandered into alien country, wears the very aspect of that old New England left far to the south and west. There are little streets of clean, white, green-shuttered houses as old as the great wine-glass elms that drip shadows down upon the roofs; there are two white churches with columned porticoes and Christopher Wren steeples, and, for the landward borders, there are the stone-walled pastures that early summer powders cheerily with buttercups and daisies.[19]

About a decade after the completion of the Robertson House, Barry contributed to the development of Dock Square, Kennebunkport as a commercial center when he remodeled the former Miller's Drugstore for its new owner, George Weinstein. The building was raised and a commercial space inserted at the lower level. As with the Robertson House, Barry was looking here at early American precedents for the decorative treatment of the building. He added a balustraded porch, cupola, and pilasters to give the store greater prominence.[20] The character of Barry's renovation underscores his reliance on historical models, but it also shows that his local practice was closely connected to the development of Kennebunkport as a summer resort of increasing popularity.

—K.D.M.   The Robertson House

The Parsons Beach Commissions, circa 1900
Kennebunk

ON OCEANFRONT PROPERTY south of the Mousam River, Charles Parsons began building a family compound in 1873. Eventually, an important group of colonial revival–style cottages and related structures was built at Crescent Surf, as the site was called, some with the assistance of Barry. By 1888 the local newspaper could report that

The Charles Parsons Cottage, Parsons Beach, Kennebunk, 1888, enlarged 1896

Perhaps no place on our coast is undergoing a more beneficial and radical change than Parson's beach, situated between the Mousam and Little rivers, and extending inland about one-half of a mile. Almost unrivaled by natural resources, owned by people possessed of means which allow the widest scope of gratification to the natural individual tastes. Thus everything is favorable for a summer resort. The Messrs. Parsons are using liberal hands to execute generous ideas. New buildings are in

William Morgan Peters, "Two Views in Reception Hall, Residence at Kennebunk, ME of Chas. Parsons, Jr., of New York," published in the *Inland Architect and News Record* (November 1890)

course of erection while others are being renovated; roads and walks laid out; trees and shrubbery of every nature cultivated; thick and bushy wood transformed into pleasant groves. On all sides luxury is fast taking the place of simplicity.[21]

One of the new buildings that were under construction at that point was the summer cottage of Charles Parsons and his wife Sarah Johnson Shepley Parsons, of New York. As a "native" of sorts (he was born in nearby Alfred, Maine in 1829) and a railroad executive and financier, Charles Parsons had an ideal background for a seacoast resort developer. In his capacity as president of the Rome, Watertown and Ogdensburg Railroad Company in New York from 1883, Parsons presided over the consolidation of a number of smaller lines. In 1891 the expanded railroad company was leased to the New York Central and Hudson River Railroad Company. Parsons was subsequently made president of the New York and New England Railroad Company. Later, he owned the South Carolina and Georgia Railroad.[22]

The Parsons house, designed by an unknown architect, was substantially altered in the course of its enlargement in 1896, but a record of its original interior is preserved in views published in 1890 in the *Inland Architect and News Record*. The cottage's exterior was a profusion of gables, dormers, railings, and towers, all characteristic of mid- to late-nineteenth–century design. One of the major rooms was the "reception hall," modeled on the "living hall" popularized by Shaw. The hall was, for both Shaw and the architect of the Parsons Cottage, more than a passage: in the Crescent Surf cottage it features an enormous hearth and a window seat, both of which would have invited use of the space as a living room. The hall is furnished with a variety of objects associated with various nineteenth-century design "movements." Asian porcelains, fans, and other objects from exotic cultures, for example, represent the wide-ranging interest of the aesthetic movement in well-designed items. Alongside these objects appear American colonial- and federal-period furnishings, including circular top tables and banister, and ribbon-back chairs.

Most of Barry's commissions at Parsons Beach further developed the colonial revival aspects of the Charles Parsons Cottage, in which the reception hall was decorated with classically detailed piers. One exception was the shingle-style Nott Cottage, which Barry designed there in 1902. Almost barnlike with its broad gambrel

William E. Barry, the Nott Cottage, Parsons Beach, Kennebunk, 1902

roof, the cottage parallels the beach and possesses little detailing. From about the same date is a more neoclassical barn that Barry expanded at Riverhurst (a house at Parsons Beach that was owned by George Parsons, who bought and expanded two connected eighteenth-century buildings there in 1885). The barn's classically derived detailing is exceptionally elaborate for an outbuilding.

The treatment of the barn is echoed in another house that Barry designed for a member of the extended Parsons family: the so-called White House, or Tennis Court House, at Parsons Beach. The house probably dates to around 1900. Barry clearly based the design on one or more of the historic houses he knew, including Wallingford Hall, where he was living at the time of the commission, or his grandfather William Lord's house, both in Kennebunk. Like many houses dating to the early Republic, the White House is rectangular in plan and surmounted by a hipped roof. The front door is designed with a fanlight above and a modified Palladian window at the second story. When the house was first built, its roof was surrounded by a balustrade (later removed) decorated with urns, further emphasizing the classicist influence.[23]

William E. Barry, the White House, or Tennis Court House, Parsons Beach, Kennebunk, circa 1900

William E. Barry, the George Parsons Barn, Parsons Beach, Kennebunk, circa 1900

Barry's project for the White House represented a quite different approach to cottage design than the one taken with the Parsons' summer residence. The irregular plan and numerous porches of the earlier building suggested informal summer living in close proximity to nature. Barry, on the other hand, used a much more pretentious and formal idiom for his design, an architectural model that had been developed by Thomas Eaton and others in the late eighteenth and early nineteenth centuries. Barry was certainly aware of the various cottage design styles employed in the seaside resorts that were developed up and down the east coast after 1850. Some of his earliest projects with Peabody & Stearns had been for Newport, Rhode Island cottages in a Queen Anne idiom, and, while working for Hartwell and Swasey in 1869, he had reported to his mother that "I am on another country house now, and have a third to do. They are quite cheap—two of them, but would be quite new for Kennebunk, as all the cheap houses in the village or about the two or three miles surrounding, are just alike."[24] The White House with its historicizing neoclassical design resembled local federal-period houses more than other cottages in the area.

—K.D.M.

The George Parsons Barn

William E. Barry, Thornton Academy Library, Saco, 1903

Thornton Academy Library, 1902
Saco

IN NOVEMBER 1901 the *Tripod*, a publication of Thornton Academy in Saco, reported that "Mrs. Annie Calef Thornton, widow of Col. Charles C. G. Thornton of Magnolia, Mass. has decided to present a new library to the academy as a memorial to her husband."[25] Charles Cutts Gookin Thornton was the grandson of Thomas G. Thornton, one of the founders of the school, and had been a student at the academy between 1839 and 1843. Although Charles Thornton had not lived in Saco, both he and his wife were from Saco families, and Col. Thornton had maintained an interest in Thornton Academy throughout his life.[26]

The commission for the library building is one of those listed by Barry in the notebook in which he recorded his architectural projects. Nonetheless, the local newspaper reported, near the time of the building's completion, that "It is a durable structure and reflects great credit on Architect H. G. Wadlin of Boston, who designed the academy building also, and on Dimon Mitchell of Biddeford, the contractor."[27] Horace G. Wadlin was actually from Reading, Massachusetts but it is true that he designed the Romanesque-revival Wadlin Hall (1888) at Thornton Academy. He was also responsible for other local buildings in the colonial revival style, including the former Dyer Library (1893) next to the Saco City Hall and the York Manufacturing Co. Agent's house (1889) on Main Street.[28] It is possible that Barry and Wadlin collaborated on the library building, or that Wadlin's name was mistakenly associated with it because of his close connection with the school and the earlier Dyer Library project.

In its form, the Thornton Academy Library is rather unlike the Dyer Library, which is more domestic in scale and detailing and whose triple-arched windows at the facade and pedimented dormer reflect eighteenth- and early nineteenth-century influences. The asymmetrical design of the Dyer Library, with its off-center door, also contrasted with the library at Thornton Academy, which follows what historian Kirk F. Mohney describes as a common pattern in public library design between the turn of the century and World War II: a three-part division of the interior is manifested on the exterior by a symmetrical elevation with an "enriched

Hutchins & French, Kennebunk Free Library, Kennebunk, 1907

pedimented entrance pavilion that projects slightly from the facade."[29] The exterior of the pavilion manifested the interior arrangement of a central circulation desk with reading rooms and book stacks to the sides.

The treatment of the neoclassical forms and details employed at the Thornton Academy Library supports the proposition that Barry designed it. For all of his attachment to neoclassicism, Barry was never orthodox or literal in his emulation of eighteenth- or early nineteenth-century buildings. This tendency was perhaps a legacy of his training in the 1860s and 1870s when interest in earlier American architecture was not an exclusive aesthetic commitment. Indeed, Barry and his mentors also championed and adopted aspects of the "free" English Queen Anne style. Thus, the portico of the Thornton Academy Library is quite different in feeling than that of the only slightly later, but much more restrained, Kennebunk Free Library (1907), designed by the Boston architectural firm of Hutchins & French. The columns on Barry's portico seem almost too widely spaced, thin, and tall in relation to the massive pediment they support.

—K.D.M.

94

Thornton Academy Headmaster's House, 1906
Saco

LIKE THE SLIGHTLY earlier library building, the Thornton Academy's headmaster's house was a gift of Annie Calef Thornton and Mary Calef Thornton in memory of Charles C. G. Thornton, Annie's husband and Mary's father. The house was completed several years after the library, prior to the start of the school year in 1906. The first headmaster to occupy the house with his family was Ernest Rolliston Woodbury, who took up the post in September 1905 and remained in it until 1937.

While the library is formal and classical in design, the headmaster's house shows a less literal interpretation of its historical influences. The house is a square, two-story mass surmounted by a hip roof. The basic concept is thus indebted to the federal-period neoclassical houses of southern Maine, some in Saco, which Barry admired. The proportions and details, however, are unique to Barry. The nearly square plan lends the building a squat appearance, which is accentuated by the very wide windows in the three-bay facade. Although the details such as balustrades and columns are inspired by federal-period houses Barry knew, the forms are put

William E. Barry, Thornton Academy Headmaster's House, Saco, 1906

Thornton Academy campus, with Headmaster's House at right, circa 1912 (top)

95

together in new ways. For instance, he uses columns in pairs and tops the center facade dormer with a broken scroll.

The interior of the building was typical of a turn-of-the-century middle-class house. As a contemporary recorded, "The hall, as you enter, impresses one by its size. It is very large and when furnished will be more like a reception room than a hall." Off the front hall, overlooking the Thornton Academy campus, was a library, appropriate to the home of the headmaster. Completing the first floor were a parlor, dining room, and kitchen with pantries. A side entrance led to a second, or back, staircase. On the second floor were five bedrooms and a sewing room, which could be converted to a bedroom. The hip roof provided useable attic space. This allocation of space corresponds to what historian Clifford Edward Clark, Jr. describes as common for the period:

> The large Victorian middle-class houses were well adapted to meeting changing patterns of family life. The sizable number of bedrooms, sometimes including a first-floor room for "sickness and age," gave the home the ability to accommodate the needs of large families with either grandparents, boarders, or newly married children. The provision of rooms that could be closed off, the proliferation of entrances and exits, the construction of front and back staircases, and the placement of outside entrances at the front, sides, and back of the house allowed individuals to come and go with a minimum of disruption.[30]

Allowing for the flexible use of space and for multiple access of rooms must have been a special priority in the house of a headmaster, where visitors would have been expected at any time.

The need for privacy would have been particularly acute as well, given that the headmaster's family was living in close proximity to his work. In general, privacy in late-Victorian houses was met not through individual rooms, as Gwendolyn Wright has suggested, but instead "was still associated with shorter periods of time alone, in a special place in the house: a window seat, a cubbyhole under the stairs, a man's library, or 'growlery.'"[31] The Thornton Academy headmaster's house had all of these spaces. Furthermore, it was equipped, at the time of its construction,

Thornton Academy Headmaster's House, hall

Thornton Academy Headmaster's House, parlor

with the domestic technologies of the day. With its dumbwaiter running from the basement to the second story, central heating, bathrooms, and laundry facilities, a contemporary account could claim that "the house is very modern and thoroughly up to date."[32] It nonetheless blended with its surroundings by recalling some of the earlier grand houses nearby in Saco.

—K.D.M.

John Calvin Stevens

JOHN CALVIN STEVENS (1855–1940) began his independent practice in 1884 when he left a partnership with Francis H. Fassett. The following four years he worked in communities in and around Portland, including Cushing's Island in Casco Bay and Delano Park in Cape Elizabeth, developing and refining his expertise in the shingle style. When the Cape Arundel commissions came into Stevens's office, from 1888 onward, he had already become well established as a leading architect in Maine.

Born in Boston, Stevens moved to Portland with his family in 1857. He trained in Fassett's office beginning in 1873 and soon rose from draftsman to junior partner, opening a Boston office on the firm's behalf in 1880. While in Boston, Stevens's office was in the same building as the office of William Ralph Emerson, whose historicist aesthetic seems to have had a profound effect on him. It was through Emerson that Stevens met Albert Winslow Cobb (1858–1941), who would become his architectural partner in 1888 (Cobb was Emerson's chief draftsman). This partnership dissolved in 1891, but both Stevens and Cobb went on to establish highly successful independent practices.[33] In 1898 Stevens took John Howard Stevens, his son, into the firm, which became Stevens Architects in 1904 when the younger Stevens was made a full partner. After the turn of the century, their firm designed private residences and many types of public buildings, such as libraries and schools, in a variety of historicist styles. John Calvin Stevens continued to prefer the shingle style and colonial revival, however.[34]

Stevens & Cobb's architecture is known for its incorporation of historical motifs as well as forms and materials that connect the buildings to the landscape. More important than the built work that represented the joint effort of the two men was their publication *Examples of American Domestic Architecture* (1888). The firm's work, as well as Stevens's independent Kennbunkport projects, suggests a special appreciation for the spectacular landscape and unique culture of Maine. As Cobb wrote in *Examples of Domestic Architecture,*

> At a time when other sections of our country are developing an evidently demoralizing luxury, there is exhibited here through out Maine a primitive simplicity and wholesome vigor of life which may serve as an object-lesson to the student of social problems.[35]

In his view the "simplicity" of Maine's architecture was to be valued not only on aesthetic grounds but for social reasons as well. Cobb posits a relationship between simple architecture and a wholesome life-style led at a remove from the perceived venality of urban culture. Except for a group of workers' cottages for the S. D. Warren paper company in Westbrook, Maine (1888), however, Stevens & Cobb's work consisted largely of projects for middle- and upper-class clients. In such instances the opportunity to effect social change was necessarily limited. But, as the firm's southern Maine commissions demonstrate, they did create designs that blended with, rather than intruded upon, the landscape and offered comfort and a place to relax to their inhabitants.

—E.G.S.

Cape Arundel Commissions, 1887–1910

JOHN CALVIN STEVENS was one of the most innovative and original architects who specialized in the design of summer cottages, and his work on Cape Arundel illustrates his considerable talents. "Though not rich in the elements which favor the accumulation of wealth and the decay of men," Stevens's partner Albert Winslow Cobb wrote, "this 'dear old Kennebunkport'—as it is now oft affectionately called—is rich in those elements which are needed to bring repose, health, sanity unto a people beginning to go mad through selfish greed."[36] Stevens & Cobb's projects in Cape Arundel offered repose to the beleaguered urbanites Cobb imagined. They also show the architects' elegant use of the varied architectural motifs that were part of the colonial revival style.

—E.G.S.

John W. Deering Cottage, or, Mizzentop, 1888–circa 1890

THE FIRST COTTAGE Stevens designed at Cape Arundel—working independently at the time—was for a prominent Portland man, Captain John W. Deering. Deering had acquired a lot from the Kennebunkport Seashore Company in November 1887.[37] Perspective sketches by Stevens for the Deering cottage, called Mizzentop, are dated January 19, 1888, and a contract for the construction of the house was signed with the Fairfield, Maine Kennebec Framing and Lumber Company in June of that year.[38]

Mizzentop was one of Stevens's most widely published designs. Even before construction began, the architect exhibited a small perspective view showing the house from the landward side at the Seventeenth Exhibition of the Portland Society of Art in May 1888. The ocean side, along with the stable, was featured in a perspective study published in *Building* in December 1888. This view, including the first-floor plan as an inset, also appeared in the 1889 book *Examples of American Domestic Architecture* by Stevens and his new partner Cobb.[39] *Scientific American, Building Edition* of November 1896 featured the house on two pages with three exterior photographs, one interior photograph, and two floor plans.[40]

John Calvin Stevens and Albert Winslow Cobb, "Sketch Study No. 1, House for Hon. John W. Deering: Kennebunkport, Me.," perspective drawing, 1889

This generous documentation allows us to compare the original designs with what was actually built. Stevens prepared two full sets of drawings, which provided alternate schemes for Deering. Perspective sketches of the executed design were labeled "Study No. 2" as published in *Examples of American Domestic Architecture*. The principal difference in the unexecuted scheme is its broader, more imposing elevation highlighted in the center with a broad oriel window above a wide frieze of floral motifs.[41] This design called for a gable roof rather than a gambrel and a single gable-roof dormer and balcony. The only noteworthy change to the interior plans appears to have been in the third story, where the original design shows a recessed porch in the gable end of the studio. It is possible that the gambrel roof design was favored as a less expensive alternative to the earlier scheme.

The house, designed in the shingle style, is compact and efficiently planned, providing the rooms with generous views in each direction. In the tradition of summer homes of the period, the plan is in the form of a main block with a kitchen wing angled off. This composition minimized obscuring scenic views from the rest of the house. An entrance into the center of the principal elevation opens directly into the living room, containing a corner fireplace, a staircase to the second floor, and two broad window seats. To the right this main room opens into a small den or reception room with its own corner fireplace. On the left, also connected by a large opening, is the dining room. The arrangement of this room fully illustrates the freedom the open plan afforded, which is expressed on the exterior in the flowing lines of the shingled skin. In plan the dining room balloons out between the main block

The John W. Deering Cottage, or Mizzentop, Kennebunkport, 1888–circa 1890, front elevation

"Stable at Kennebunkport, Me., for John W. Deering, Esq.," circa 1888, front elevation

of the house and the kitchen wing, maximizing its exposure to light and air. The kitchen wing, with a butler's closet, pantry, and servants' porch, is joined to a back service hall. On the second floor were five bedrooms for the family, two for servants, and a bathroom, each room with at least two windows positioned for views. The third floor contained a billiard room in the tower, a studio in the gable end, and another bedroom.

The wood-shingled exterior is the unifying feature of the design. The house is covered by a gambrel roof extending down to the first floor with broad overhanging eaves. The dining room is part of a round tower linked to the main block and capped by a third-floor lookout with a conical roof. Twin hip dormers connected by a balcony with a shingled railing, overlook the steps leading to the main entrance. The house features a fieldstone foundation forming an open piazza on one side, with a shingled railing, that extends from the corner tower across the principal elevation. The piazza continues beneath the second-floor gambrel-roof overhang above the reception room, reemerging in the open to extend across a portion of the rear facade. This masterful composition was a perfect solution for a compact, yet architecturally distinguished summer cottage.

Also built for Captain Deering was a small shingle-style stable, now unfortunately demolished, which resembled a small seventeenth-century dwelling; the wing with animal stalls featured a saltbox profile. With its steeply pitched gables and gambrel roof, the building recalled the early vernacular architecture nearby.

When John W. Deering built his Cape Arundel cottage he had already lived an extraordinary and active life. Born in Saco in 1833, Deering went to sea at age sixteen, rising to become a captain of merchant ships that sailed to Europe and China. In 1867 he settled in Portland, where his firm, the Deering Winslow Company, imported southern pine. He served as an alderman and mayor of Portland, first as a Republican and later as a Democrat. As mayor he played a major role in the creation of the city's park system. Mizzentop was his summer residence for nearly fifteen years. He died in 1904.[42]

—E.G.S.

Mizzentop, front elevation (top left), side and rear elevations (top right), and main hall (above)

The Ellen K. Brazier Cottage, or Juniper Ledge, 1891

WHILE THE DEERING COTTAGE was the work of Stevens himself, two other Cape Arundel cottages were by the firm of Stevens & Cobb.[43] Juniper Ledge was designed for Mrs. Ellen K. Brazier of Philadelphia, who, with Joseph Brazier, had acquired lots on Cape Arundel in September 1888. The main block of the Brazier cottage is of a familiar colonial type, a two-and-a-half story structure with a gable roof. At one end is a large verandah that wraps around on the ocean side. A porte cochere with paired Tuscan columns extends over the main entrance, below Stevens's characteristic twin gable-roof dormers. More unusual is the servants' wing, which projects from one end of the house toward the driveway. Here a steeply pitched gable roof extends down to just above the first-floor level, suggestive of a seventeenth-century farmhouse. Stevens borrowed the design for the gable-roof dormer with balcony located on the roof of this wing from the preliminary plans of his earlier Deering cottage.

A period photograph shows a large open living hall on the first floor with a staircase and corner fireplace, and an adjoining room for a den.[44] A porch in the

Stevens & Cobb, the Ellen K. Brazier Cottage, or Juniper Ledge, Kennebunkport, 1891

Juniper Ledge, living hall

rear offered views over a long, sloping lawn. The cottage blended with its environment because of its naturalistic materials, which included fieldstone and wood shingles, and its historical referents, but also as a consequence of the extensive landscaping. Vines almost obscured all architectural features except the porches.

Juniper Ledge had an interesting offshoot in the form of another commission for Stevens. In 1896 Richard Cheney of South Manchester, Connecticut, saw a photograph of the cottage in a magazine advertisement and asked if Stevens could design something similar for him. An undated sketch by the architect shows a design for a suburban dwelling that is similar but with significant alterations to the pattern of window openings on the exterior and the substitution of an entrance porch with a full pediment for the porte cochere on the Brazier cottage.[45]

—E.G.S.

The Robert S. Smith Cottage, or Kenridge Cottage, 1891

AT THE SAME TIME that the Brazier cottage was being built, Stevens & Cobb had a house underway for Robert S. Smith of Columbus, Ohio, who was treasurer of the Columbus & Xenier Railroad.[46] The Kenridge Cottage is L-shaped in plan, with the traditional porch extending around two sides. The floor plans and perspective sketch for this project are in mirror plan to what was actually built.[47] Although sheathed in wood shingles, the house lacks the sense of a seamless exterior associated with the shingle style. Elements such as the gable roof with projecting eaves, porches, and windows with blinds are all sharply delineated, lending the house a more colonial revival character.[48]

Stevens & Cobb, the Robert
S. Smith Cottage, or
Kenridge Cottage,
Kennebunkport, 1891

The floor plan for Kenridge was as linear as the exterior. A large central hall forms the center room, with a separate staircase hall against the rear wall. On either side of the hall is a dining room and a small office. Built on a high rock outcropping, near the easternmost point of Cape Arundel, the cottage enjoys a sweeping view, especially from the second-story bedrooms. A small center porch at that level provides an outlook to Kennebunk Beach at the south, and Cape Porpoise at the north.

—E.G.S.

Kenridge Cottage, plan

Kenridge Cottage, perspective sketch, 1891

The Erskine H. Bronson Cottage, or Bonnie Brae, 1895–96

FOLLOWING SHORTLY ON the design of the Brazier cottage was a project for Erskine Henry Bronson, who purchased two lots at Cape Arundel, one on Old Fort Avenue in October 1892 and another on the corner of Summit and Atlantic avenues just a year later. Although born in the United States, Bronson was from Ottawa, Canada. He was president of the Bronson-Weston lumber company and was also associated with other firms. A letter from Bronson to Stevens dated September 7, 1895 indicates that it was not until that time that construction estimates for the house were obtained.[49] Bonnie Brae was probably built during the winter of 1895 to 1896.

Documentation for the original appearance of this altered house suggests that it was designed in the shingle style with Stevens's characteristic twin-gable roofs flanking a second-story porch on the principal facade. The verandah across the front of the house was rather shallow for a summer cottage, as the original house appears to have been small and compact. Wings now extend from two sides of the house, and the porches have been enclosed with glazing.

—E.G.S.

John Calvin Stevens, the Erskine H. Bronson Cottage, or Bonnie Brae, Kennebunkport, 1983, front elevation

The Edwin Packard Cottage, or Braemar Cottage, 1897

AT THE SAME TIME as the Moss cottage was being designed (see p. 110), Stevens was working on a summer house for Brooklyn resident Edwin Packard, who was vice president and director of the Federal Mining and Smelting Company located in New York City.[53] The design for Braemar Cottage was much more in the spirit of Stevens's earlier shingle-style cottages. Although the house, which still exists, employs several more traditional colonial revival–style motifs such as Palladian windows, the dominant feature is the broad expanse of shingled cross-gabled gambrel roofs encompassing the volume of the house. These roofs sweep down to the first story, forming part of the roof for a verandah on the ocean facade. Each elevation presents a different fenestration pattern: Oriel windows, Palladian windows, and double-hung sash, arranged on their own or in groups of two or three, provide an abundance of light as well as highly varied facades. Unfortunately, no plans are available to appreciate how Stevens organized the rooms.

—E.G.S.

John Calvin Stevens, the Edwin Packard Cottage, or Braemar, Kennebunkport, 1897

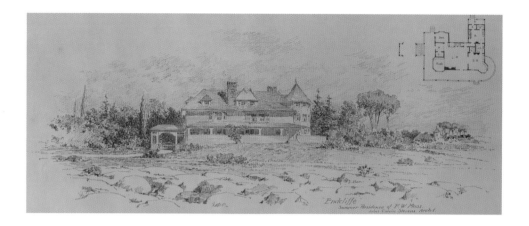

The Frederick W. Moss Cottage, or Endcliffe, 1897–circa 1899

THROUGH THE SECOND HALF of the 1890s, Stevens continued to execute designs for Cape Arundel cottages.[50] Frederick W. Moss, an importer and manufacturer of steel files and tools from Brooklyn, New York, acquired his Ocean Avenue land in two parcels, in November 1895 and September 1897.[51] A rendering of his cottage, Endcliffe, by Stevens with a small first floor plan was produced in the same year.[52] Construction probably began during the winter of 1897 to 1898.

The design for the Moss cottage is in the shingle style, but some elements, such as the double-gable facade flanked by a chimney, suggest the influence of the arts and crafts movement as well. Like at Kenridge Cottage, the shingled exterior of Endcliffe is employed more as a practical necessity for an oceanfront house than as an integrated element in the design. In contrast to the extruded dining room tower of Juniper Ledge, Endcliffe's corner tower is awkwardly attached to the house at one end in a manner that is more typical of contractor-built houses of the period. Window sash with ornamental muntin patterns, heavy square porch posts with ogee-shaped brackets, and a porte cochere contribute to a more formal, suburban character, causing the house to stand out from its neighbors. The plan, however, is that of a traditional ninetee th-century summer cottage, with a large living hall providing central circulatio to smaller satellite rooms.

—E.G.S.

John Calvin Stevens, "Endcliffe, Summer Residence of F. W. Moss, John Calvin Stevens, Arch't.," circa 1897, perspective sketch

Kennebunkport, Me., Cape Arundel.

Endcliffe, postcard, circa
1900 (top) and photograph,
circa 1910

The Gideon Walker House, 1745

additions and alterations, 1910

John Calvin Stevens, the
Gideon Walker House,
Kennebunkport, 1745, as
remodeled in 1910 (top) and
prior to remodeling (above)

THE LAST STEVENS project in Kennebunkport is pure colonial revival rather than shingle style and continues the tradition of working with motifs derived from vernacular architecture. Anson McKim of Montreal, Canada, owner of the advertising agency, A. McKim and Company, bought the Gideon Walker House on Cape Arundel together with his wife, Bessie, in 1907. Three years later they hired the Stevens firm to design a new town house in Montreal and to remodel their Maine farmhouse.[54]

Built in 1745, the Walker House was a traditional rural dwelling almost bereft of architectural ornament. Although the addition doubled the size of the building, the simple vernacular character of the old farmhouse was maintained by Stevens. The front of the original house was five bays wide with a central chimney and faced the street with an enclosed entrance portico that was probably added in the early nineteenth century. The rear facade faced an open yard in front of a barn that extended perpendicularly

112

The Gideon Walker House, parlor and dining room

to the house. While preserving the existing two-and-a-half-story house, Stevens designed a wing of almost the same size and dimensions on the former site of the barn, which had since been removed. A long porch—partially open, partially screened, and partially glazed—extends across the rear facade of the old house and continues around two sides of the new wing. This design adapted the old building to its new use by providing spaces in which to enjoy the landscape. While benefiting from their new openness to the exterior, the rooms of the old house retained their eighteenth-century character with low ceilings and antique furnishings. The simplicity of the addition is completely in character with the old Maine farmhouse and fits well into the Kennebunkport summer colony.

All of Stevens's clients would no doubt have agreed with his former partner Cobb, who wrote, "It is indeed refreshing to escape awhile from some huge, overgrown metropolis and to steep one's self in the sedative influence of such a place as Kennebunkport."[55] Like other architects who had been inspired by William Ralph Emerson, Stevens adapted historical models to new requirements in a variety of ways. Despite their varied approaches, Stevens's Cape Arundel designs all provided just the right environments in which to enjoy the refreshing escape Kennebunkport offered.

—E.G.S.

John Calvin Stevens and John Howard Stevens, York Institute, Saco, 1926

York Institute, 1926
Saco

MIDDLE-CLASS DOMESTIC LIFE and the American home, especially the colonial American home, were firmly established as preeminent social virtues in the years following World War I. This longing for domesticity was translated into popular architecture as well. Although designed as a museum, the building for the York Institute, erected in 1926, perfectly reflected these ideals, both in its design and in the exhibits it housed.[56] The 1920s in America are well known for the cultural projects many wealthy men instigated, fighting a vigorous rearguard action against the social changes that they themselves were largely responsible for bringing about. Henry Ford, whose inexpensive cars provided mobility to the common man—bringing dramatic change to the traditional values of rural America—constructed Greenfield Village in 1928 to commemorate an idealized vision of the past. Prior to that, in 1924, Ford had purchased and "restored" the Wayside Inn in Sudbury, Massachusetts as a working tavern, memorializing one aspect of America's colonial heritage. Ford is the best-known example as his wealth allowed him to recreate large and well-publicized memorials to preindustrial America. Communities all over the country established museums to honor early American history, often simply by amassing large collections of artifacts in one building. The York Institute in Saco already had a long history of collecting and exhibiting artifacts before constructing its new museum in 1926.

Saco in the 1920s typified the change industrialization had brought to old communities. By the mid-nineteenth century, the twin cities of Saco and Biddeford formed one of the principal industrial centers of Maine. Their population had radically changed in the nineteenth century, first with the Irish who came in large numbers after 1850, and then with the French Canadians who were attracted by work in the towns' textile mills. By 1900 over half the population was French speaking. In the face of this change the Yankee heritage of Saco was fast disappearing. The establishment of the York Institute in 1866 was intended to educate the new citizens of the town about local history and culture. At first the emphasis was primarily on education through lectures since the institute had little space to exhibit objects. This changed as the institute moved, first to an old counting house on Factory Island and then, in 1890, into the Sweetser Block on Main Street. With three floors in this building, greater importance could be given to the display of artifacts celebrating early American culture.

The turn-of-the-century museums dedicated to the history and culture of colonial America typically collected and displayed artifacts with little control over quantity or presentation. The most popular room for display was usually the kitchen with its large bake oven and fireplace filled with utensils. This room, above all, became emblematic of the American colonial revival. In many ways the York Institute's 1926 building represented the most progressive approach in an effort to rationalize the architecture for what had become a mania for museums of early American heritage.

A bequest made in 1890 had enabled the York Institute to purchase the Sweetser Block in Saco. On one floor was a 380-seat auditorium demonstrating the importance of educational programs for the institute. Initially, programs on science and art were considered no less important than history. The building included a museum room to display natural history, an art room for paintings, and a library. It also featured rooms devoted to what were described as "domestic manufacturers," an "old-fashioned kitchen," and an "old-fashioned bedroom." Indeed, the York Institute was among the earliest organizations in New England to follow the novel concept of a period room rather than a room full of a mixture of objects. It was through these rooms, and its invitation to the public to contribute objects, that the York Institute began to change the emphasis of its mission. Rather than serving to promote science, art, and history, its purpose increasingly came to focus on the latter. President Harding had called for a return to "normalcy" after World War I, and the mission of the York Institute came to emphasize the ideals commonly associated with that ill-defined word.

The construction of a new building was made possible by a bequest of $40,000 from Henrietta Pierce Watkinson of California. The money was donated in memory of her father, Marshall Pierce, who had been a strong supporter of the York Institute before moving to California. The trustees hired the architects John

Calvin Stevens and John Howard Stevens, and supervised the construction from start to finish. Work began in May 1926 and was largely completed by the end of the year.

The York Institute was constructed in brick, primarily as a fireproofing measure. Even though wood was traditionally the most common building material in New England, brick also provided a strong association with eighteenth-century architecture. With a high basement, stone water table, and two brick end-wall chimneys—features historically associated with southern climates—the Stevens firm acknowledged a national rather than New England standard for the popular image of colonial architecture.

The design of the entrance, however, pays homage to a predominantly New England feature: it is the traditional single door of late-eighteenth– and early-nineteenth–century vernacular buildings of the type popularized in the builders' guides by Asher Benjamin. A fanlight with a decorative muntin pattern surmounts the single door, which is framed by pilasters supporting a pediment. The use of vernacular molding profiles continued in the York Institute's interior with doors, moldings, and fireplace mantels. That the architectural origin of these details was post-Revolutionary rather than colonial mattered little, if only because the first settlement period of the early Republic held, by the 1920s, an equal place of honor in American history.

The York Institute was different from Stevens's other museum design, the L. D. Sweat Memorial for the Portland Society of Art of 1911. That project was an art gallery, although it was attached to a historic house museum. In terms of its design and function, the York Institute has more in common with the firm's small library designs. These buildings varied greatly in style, however; the one that bears most similarity to the York Institute is the South Paris Public Library constructed in the same year. It is smaller with a hip roof, and the detailing is less refined, but the basic plan of a central rectangular block with a perpendicular rear wing for book stacks is the same. Another Stevens library that is similar in spirit to the York Institute is the one in Bethel of 1937 to 1938. Although a wood building and smaller even than the one in Paris, this library conveys a strong sense of the domestic quality that is characteristic of the York building. Architectural

York Institute

detailing used at the Bethel Library was also derived from the period of the early Republic.

The interior of the York Institute continues the blend of residential and institutional characteristics conveyed by its exterior. A central hall is flanked by two large rooms with fireplaces. These exhibit rooms are spacious with tall ceilings and large, round arched windows, as the intention was not to recreate the often cramped dimensions of a period house at the expense of the exhibit space. Directly on axis to the front entrance is the door to the rear ell. Originally used as a library with book stacks, it now contains gallery spaces, which are well lit with a tall ceiling and triple-hung sash. On the second floor are two smaller rooms, one serving as a meeting room for the board of directors and the other as an additional exhibit space.

Of particular interest to the public was the basement, where the period kitchen was located. The architects played a direct role in the design of this space, producing a sketch with the fireplace and bake oven; sink with hand pump; and a ceiling beam, a structural feature found in seventeenth-century timber-frame architecture. There were numerous models for the architects to draw from, including the kitchens of the Old York Goal and the Wadsworth-Longfellow House in Portland. The kitchen had been the principal symbol of the colonial revival as early as at the Centennial Exhibition in Philadelphia in 1876. Indeed, the colonial kitchen had been featured in the popular press for so many years that by 1926 its idealized image was firmly planted in the mind of the average citizen.

PUBLIC LIBRARY, SOUTH PARIS, MAINE.

John Calvin Stevens and John Howard Stevens, Public Library, South Paris, 1926

John Calvin Stevens had grown up surrounded by enough real colonial houses to know that his version of the colonial kitchen was a heavily varnished presentation. As historian Kerry O'Brien has observed in her study of the York Institute:

> Celebrating domesticity, the kitchen was an icon of the past and, by the 1930s, a popular convention in historical museums. As a colonial symbol, the kitchen most powerfully transported the visitor back in time. The kitchen brought together many romantic threads of the "colonial": the stability of family life, the comforts of home, simplicity, hard work and perseverance on the frontier.[57]

The York Institute as originally built represented an image of early American history that its builders wished to convey. It would not be until the late twentieth century that curators would begin to strive for a truer representation of America's past.

—R. R.

Henry Paston Clark

THE COMMISSIONS OF William E. Barry, William Ralph Emerson, and John Calvin Stevens notwithstanding, Henry Paston Clark (1853–1927) was essentially the resident architect for the summer colony in Kennebunkport. Landmarks to his credit include such public buildings for the summer community as the Colony Hotel, the Arundel Casino, and a host of small and large cottages along the bank of the Kennebunk River and at Cape Arundel.

Clark was brought up on Beacon Hill in Boston, the son of Dr. Henry Grafton Clark, the prominent city physician and inspector-in-chief of army hospitals for the U.S. Sanitary Commission during the Civil War. The family had deep roots in the Kennebunks; Portsmouth, New Hampshire; and Lexington, Massachusetts; and had owned a number of early American houses that were of antiquarian interest by the 1870s. Clark's ancestry was central to his identity and inspired his strong affinity with the colonial revival, which was gaining momentum in his youth. He revered his forebears, whom he considered to be among the "true Americans," and treasured family heirlooms such as the gateleg table of his great-grandfather, the Reverend Jonas Clarke of Lexington, who was locally important in Revolutionary history. Dr. Clark was a member of the Massachusetts State Centennial Board and participated in Lexington commemorations of the events of 1775. Henry Paston Clark pursued his father's historical interests by submitting a *Sketch for Mass. State Building* to the building committee for the Philadelphia Exhibition of 1876.[58]

Clark's grandfather, Henry Clark, had come from Lexington to Kennebunkport during the height of the shipbuilding era. The architect's father had been brought up there, and his sister Susan had married a Clark relative in Kennebunkport. The development of the summer resort represented a significant career opportunity for the young architect. There were hotels, social institutions, and cottages to be built, and Henry Paston Clark was there from the beginning to design them.

Taking a path that was typical of Boston architects of the period, he studied architecture at the MIT from 1870 to 1871 and subsequently worked as a draftsman in Boston at 18 Pemberton Square, possibly for architects Nathaniel Bradlee, George

F. Fuller, or A. C. Martin, all of whom had offices there. He went on to study in Paris, where, in 1874, he was listed in the atelier of Louis-Jules André, who was associated with the Ecole de Beaux-arts.[59] Clark's first hotel in Kennebunkport, the Parker House, built in 1878,[60] brought the waning influence of the French Second Empire style to the summer resort. Being located in town next to the Congregational Church, it was appropriately more formal than contemporary hotels built closer to the shore.[61] Clark quickly found his own voice amidst the spirit of the times when the distinctly American shingle style was emerging.

Draftsman John Russell (1851–1936) joined Clark's practice in 1883, during Clark's short-lived partnership with Ion Lewis, who joined the New York firm of McKim, Mead & White in 1885. Clark also briefly collaborated with Henry Vaughan, the influential English Gothicist, from 1889 to 1891.[62] Clark and Russell became partners in 1899 and practiced together into the 1920s. Beyond Kennebunkport, built works and designs attributed to Clark include hotels, houses, Episcopal churches, meeting halls, and libraries in the Boston suburbs and along the coast from Hyannisport, Massachusetts to New Brunswick, Canada.

The central theme of his practice was the adaptation of regional vernacular colonial architecture to the informality of modern summer life. He worked with the basic forms of the gambrel roof and the lean-to, the pitched roof and the hip, the shingled skin, and rock foundations, and then opened up the walls with porches that both penetrated into the masses of the houses and flowed out into the landscape. Clark also employed naturalistic elements such as sea stone, which climbed up shingled walls like ivy or was used in porches and steps.

Queen Anne elements on the exteriors of some of his buildings, such as oriel windows, half-timbered gable ends, or crenellation on stone or wooden bays were freely combined with colonial revival motifs in the interiors, such as staircases and balustrades, white walls, paneling, and mantelpieces.

In his later work, Clark moved away from the relative informality of his Kennebunkport designs. His development toward neoclassical formality corresponded with the architectural shift that emerged in the late 1880s, enunciated in the World's Columbian Exposition at Chicago in 1893. Examples in Clark & Russell's work include the Hyde Park Library (1898) in Boston and conservative

Georgian-revival houses in Brookline, an affluent suburb of Boston. The firm's continuing commissions for summer houses in Kennebunkport and elsewhere in the late 1890s and early 1900s were often large buildings for wealthy clients.

—K.L.

Kennebunkport Commissions (1878–1916)

EARLY WORKS

Clark's early Kennebunkport projects show distinctly how the shingle style evolved from vernacular buildings. One example is the Bunk, a boathouse Clark built for himself on the bank of the Kennebunk River as a humble retreat and a place to hang his scull. The house invoked the lean-to roof, a colonial vernacular form, but it was cleanly penetrated by a cut-out for a porch. A succinct early design using the colonial gambrel roof is the L-shaped F. W. Sprague Cottage by Clark and Ion Lewis, published in 1882.[63] The roof here flows over the porch, however, and the living and dining areas are combined into one space. In the same vein is the Arundel House, a relaxed gambrel-roofed boarding house built along the river for Miss Alice and Ida Paine of Boston between 1884 and 1885, which is today the Breakwater Inn on Ocean Avenue.

On the flat riverbank behind the Bunk, Clark built a group of modest speculative cottages that survive today with numerous additions he designed for various owners. Among them was Greywood (or Greylock), an awkward version of a small early Georgian house of three bays with a gambrel roof and center doorway; it was enlarged for Margaret and Lorin Deland around 1890 to 1892, and published in 1895 as a house "in the Colonial style" with "picturesque perspective."[64] Margaret Deland was a popular author who often wrote nostalgically on historical subjects and could thus have been expected to have appreciated Clark's aesthetic.

—K.L.

Henry Paston Clark, Margaret Deland Cottage, Greywood (or Greylock), Kennebunkport, 1890–92

Arundel Casino, 1886

A GROUP OF EARLY summer residents, led by Sarah P. Bancroft of Boston (for whom Clark & Lewis had designed a cottage in 1883), founded the Arundel Casino to serve as a social gathering place for the nascent summer community. The building was designed by Clark in 1886 and included a hall for theatrical entertainments, a reading room, a dormitory for bachelors, and tennis courts. Clark's talent for picturesque massing is epitomized by the Arundel Casino, originally situated near the Colony Hotel. The building was later moved to Ocean Avenue and incorporated into the Kennebunk River Club. The earlier parts of the building were somewhat reorganized in the new location.

The Casino illustrates how Clark had absorbed the sense of place that attracted people to Kennebunkport. In his design he adapts elements of the local vernacular, such as the additive informality of the wharves on the river with their straightforward windows set in a plain wooden skin. The long hall evokes the historic Maling rigging

Henry Paston Clark,
Arundel Casino,
Kennebunkport, 1886

Arundel Casino, later moved and altered

loft in Kennebunkport, which had a single gable and small twelve-over-twelve pane windows. The Palladian window on the Casino facade and the Georgian-style balustrade of the porte cochere are formal neoclassical elements, typical of the colonial revival, that contrast with the more picturesque stone piers and projecting tower of the building.

In its deliberate austerity the Casino epitomizes the distinction between Kennebunkport and other resorts of its time: The formal simplicity of the building reflects the more socially relaxed atmosphere of Kennebunkport. The building can be contrasted with the more ostentatious shingle-style casinos designed by the New York architectural firm of McKim, Mead & White at Newport, Rhode Island (1879–81); Short Hills, New Jersey (1882–83); and the Narragansett Pier, also in Rhode Island (1881–84). While Clark's building, like those of McKim, Mead & White, incorporates neoclassical and Queen Anne motifs, it is smaller in scale, and elaborate details never overwhelm its ultimately vernacular quality.

—K.L.

Arundel Casino

Henry Paston Clark, the Charles H. Manning Cottage, Kennebunkport, 1887

The Charles H. Manning Cottage, 1887

BUILT NEAR CLARK'S OWN boathouse on the riverbank, the Charles H. Manning Cottage displays the architect's dexterity in adapting a powerful colonial image to an informal, open-air lifestyle. Like the Bunk, the Manning Cottage has the massing of a lean-to house. When it was published in *Scientific American Building Edition* in 1895, it was characterized as "picturesque" and "most unique."[65] The article went on to say of the cottage:

> It is designed after the old "New England" lean-to roof order, giving all the apartments on two floors, with low ceilings and large, open fireplaces. The principal feature of the exterior is the bay-window, chimney and underpinning, built of rock-faced fieldstone laid up at random. The remainder of the exterior is built of wood and covered with shingles, and stained mahogany color.[66]

With this design, Clark referred to historical architecture—through the lean-to roof—while underscoring the importance of the landscape to summer residents—through the use of porches facing the river and the stone tower.

Clark's client, Charles H. Manning, was general superintendent of the Amoskeag Manufacturing Company in Manchester, New Hampshire. Founded in the early nineteenth century, the Amoskeag Company was the largest textile producer in the world by the time of World War I. The company had 17,000 employees, working in nearly three dozen mill buildings, who collectively produced nearly fifty miles of finished cloth every hour. The company's foundry manufactured locomotives and firearms, among other products, during the Civil War.[67] Charles Manning was known for having designed the Manning boiler, widely used in textile manufacturing.[68]

—K.L.

St. Anns by the Sea,
Kennebunkport, Me.

Henry Paston Clark, St. Ann's Church, Kennebunkport, 1887–92, postcard, circa 1900

St. Ann's Church, 1887–92

EQUALLY WELL INTEGRATED into its setting through the use of naturalistic materials is St. Ann's Church, which was built as the Episcopal chapel for the summer
colony at Kennebunkport. It is Clark's most admired building and represents the
essence of his personal style. Clark was instrumental in St. Ann's founding and
was a constant presence at the church; his great-granddaughter recounted that he
spent most of his Sundays there and was a long-time treasurer and vestry member.[69] Clark also guided the embellishment of the church with artwork. Published
notices after Clark's death considered St. Ann's as the building he would be
remembered for, a monument to his life's work.[70]

In his design for the church, Clark embraced vernacular simplicity and a con-
trolled picturesque aesthetic. St. Ann's composition harkens back to the seventeenth-
century rural Anglican church in the colonies and a distant, romanticized image
of the rural English parish church. In 1884 *American Architect and Building News*
published a photograph of the Old Brick Church in Isle of Wight County
Virginia, built in the 1630s. This early church has a three-story tower and nave
shaped almost exactly like Clark's design for St. Ann's published in the *American
Architect and Building News* in 1887. The jagged and weathered basaltic sea stones
of which St. Ann's was built were picked from the site, lending the exterior its
deep tones of gray, purple, and green. They were trimmed with curved buttresses
and appropriately matched with a slate roof. A period description of St. Ann's
emphasized the visual connection between the exterior and interior: "Inside and

Cape Arundel with
St. Ann's Church at right,
photograph, circa 1890

St. Ann's Church, nave interior

out are alike of stone, and the altar is of square stones, porphyry and agate, and others polished and set with the accuracy of a mosaic."[71] These picturesque and naturalistic elements are complemented by historicist features; oak hammer-beam trusses dominate the interior.[72]

—K.L.

St. Ann's Church

Breakwater Court, 1914

Henry Paston Clark,
Breakwater Court, now
the Colony Hotel,
Kennebunkport, 1914

A DIFFERENT VEIN of the colonial revival, the more formal classicism derived from Georgian architecture of the late eighteenth century, was much less important in Clark's work than in the designs of his counterpart, William E. Barry. Some of Clark's designs are nonetheless neoclassical, including Breakwater Court, later known as the Colony Hotel, which was the largest project undertaken by Clark & Russell. The complex could accommodate 250 guests, and was comprised of kitchen and laundry buildings, staff housing, and a large auto garage. It occupied the site of the first hotel built on Cape Arundel, the Ocean Bluff of 1873, which had burned down in 1898. In its imposing formality, Breakwater Court illustrated class consciousness in a village that was rooted in rural simplicity with democratic illusions. The design fulfilled the vision of the client, Ruel W. Norton, an ambitious Kennebunkport hotelkeeper who had the goal of catering to "the most fastidious class of patronage"—the bluebloods of New York, Boston, and other "society centers."[73]

The models for this monumental colonial revival hotel lie in collegiate architecture of the late-eighteenth century, a style that Clark & Vaughan had employed in their design for the Lower School at St. Paul's School in 1891. The dominant central projecting portico, the build-ing's conception as a solid rectangular block of three or more stories, and its low-pitched roof and dormers are characteristic features of large forms. The portico may have been inspired, among other sources, by Mount Vernon (George Washington's house), an important prototype for the colonial revival since the first campaign for its preserva-tion in the 1850s.[74]

Breakwater Court, postcard, circa 1920

The Judge Jonas Clark House (also known as the William Lord mansion) on Summer Street in Kennebunk is a possible local influence on the pilasters and dormers of the facade. Henry Paston Clark was impressed by the house as an architectural achievement of his great-uncle. The Jonas Clark House was also an ancestral home for architect William Barry, who published it in his *Pen Sketches of Old Houses* (1874). Clark wrote on the first page of his family's genealogy that "There is a picture of his [Judge Jonas Clark's] house at Kennebunk, which is the finest example of a Colonial mansion there, in the *White Pine Series of Architectural Monographs* Vol. IV–No. 2."[75] Breakwater Court expresses the reverse of the freedom that characterized Clark's vernacular idiom of the 1880s. Yet it was successful in achieving the client's goal and still serves as an elite resort to this day.

—K.L.

Bayberry Cove, 1915–16

CLARK'S FINAL DESIGN for a summer house on Cape Arundel—Bayberry Cove, built between 1915 and 1916 on speculation and purchased by Emma (Mrs. James) Harrison of Brookline, Massachusetts—effectively integrated historical and natural references. The rugged rock foundation growing organically out of the surf-beaten site strives toward a complete integration with the landscape, similar to St. Ann's Church. Basically a cross-gabled shingled mass, the cottage presents a profusion of gables and rooflines to the street, suggesting a building that has grown over time. Perched atop a rock outcropping on the shore, Bayberry Cove faces the ocean with porches and a balcony. Dramatic views can be enjoyed from every side.[76] Indeed, an advertisement for the cottage emphasized the amenity represented by the porch on the ocean side:

> On the capacious front piazza of this cottage on a hot summer's day comes cool, continuous, refreshing breezes to fan one's cheeks when all around, in city and town, is sweltering heat. Especially delightful to the senses is a warm evening spent on this piazza, when the full moon, shining brightly, is an early and late evening visitor, casting its silvery, shimmering path across the broad ocean up to, seemingly, this identical cottage, and none other.[77]

The house had on the first floor, a "parlor, hall and reception room all in one, so to speak, divided only by portieres," creating a flow of living spaces. The second story housed five bedrooms, three of which directly faced the ocean. With an additional three bedrooms on the third story, and a servant's bedroom over the laundry, the house was equipped to handle a large family with a live-in staff.[78]

With its darkly picturesque, mysterious aura, the cottage recalls colonial revival imagery of the seventeenth century. Like the vernacular houses that Clark and other architects of his generation admired, Bayberry Cove seems to ramble across the landscape with its connected, but visually distinctive, parts.

—K.L.

Henry Paston Clark, Bayberry Cove cottage, Kennebunkport, 1915–16

Arthur Little OF LITTLE & BROWNE

ARTHUR LITTLE (1852–1925) was born in Boston in 1852 to James Lovell and Julia Augusta Cook Little. He studied at MIT intermittently in the 1870s; Little appears to have been a student there at the same time that he was apprenticing with Peabody & Stearns, in 1876. While working as a draftsman for the firm, Little, with his Peabody & Stearns colleagues, began recording surviving eighteenth-century

Arthur Little, J. G. Thorp House, Cambridge, 1889

Arthur Little, renovations to the Emmerton House, Salem, 1885

architecture. His efforts culminated in the publication of *Early New England Interiors* in 1878.[79] With his first three independent projects—the renovation of the G. R. Emmerton House in Salem in 1885, the design of the Georgian-inspired Joseph Thorp House in Cambridge in 1889, and the design of his own house in Boston's Back Bay neighborhood around 1890,[80] Little affirmed his neoclassical leanings and established an architectural practice that offered both house and furnishing design. A contemporary wrote of Arthur Little's own house that

> [Number 2 Raleigh St.] is most remarkable, being constructed of material taken from a number of old colonial houses, some parts being upwards of two hundred years old, the whole forming a most unique and artistic combination and a noble evidence of Mr. Little's architectural skill.[81]

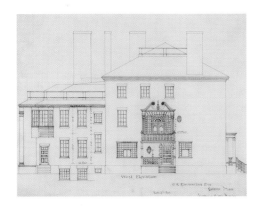

Renovation to the Emmerton House,
west elevation

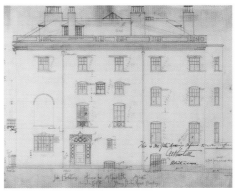

Arthur Little, Arthur Little House, Boston,
circa 1890, side elevation

Arthur Little, "Waters
House, Parlor Chimney-
Piece," from *Early New
England Interiors* (1878)

Indeed, the house was an exuberant summation of the architect's development during the 1870s and 1880s. The design was restrained on the exterior, and historian Bainbridge Bunting considered it "one of four houses erected in 1890 which uses the federal style with fidelity."[82] On the interior, the house illustrated Little's wide-ranging design interests. He incorporated fragments of historic buildings into the design, reusing, for example, a mantelpiece and doorway lintels ornamented with swags of flowers, which he had salvaged from the Perez Morton House in Roxbury. Designed by Charles Bulfinch, and built in 1796, the Perez Morton House was demolished around 1890.[83] The interior of Little's house was in no way uniformly "colonial" in feeling, however. Little's respect for earlier American material culture reflected a broader sensibility; he also showed an affinity for the aesthetic and arts and crafts movements. A period photo shows the walls covered in the Wandle fabric designed by William Morris, a leader of the arts and crafts movement, in 1884. This printed cotton, as well as Morris's Honeysuckle (1876), used as a throw for the daybed,[84] is here incorporated into a room with an elaborately detailed fireplace wall of Little's design, based on Georgian models.

Little shared an interest not only in colonial architecture but also in early furnishings with his close associates. Herbert Browne (1860–1946), who was Little's architectural partner from 1890; the architect Ogden Codman, Jr.; and Little were known collectively within the social circle as the "Colonial Trinity."[85]

Arthur Little House, parlor

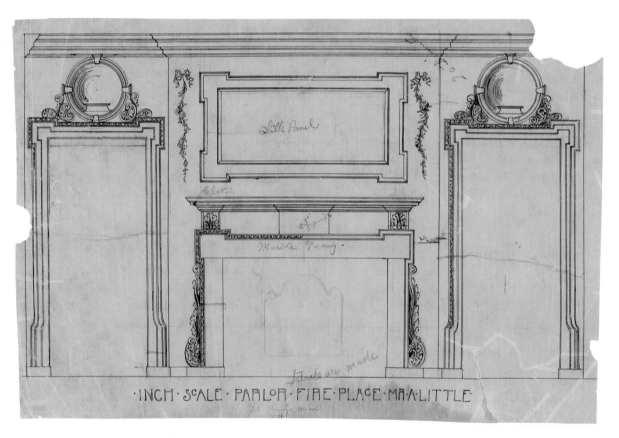

Arthur Little, "Inch Scale Parlor Fire Place [for] Mr. A. Little," pen and ink drawing, circa 1890

Yet none of them was exclusive in his architectural tastes. Little, in particular, was drawn to the art and architecture of Italy where he traveled often and acquired furnishings for himself and clients. He admired the ancient Greek temples of Sicily, the Rococo architecture of Palermo, and the Renaissance palaces of Florence. Indeed, he was so enraptured by Italy that he claimed to Codman in 1892 that "Some one wants to buy #2 Raleigh St! Fancy I should sell it for a good price and build another only I should have no Colonial things and should have to have it Italian."[86] Little nonetheless continued to use colonial motifs and furnishings in his commissions with Browne. But he incorporated Italian-inspired architectural forms and furnishings from Italy in various projects, including his own later (circa 1910) house in Beverly Farms, Massachusetts. Called Spartavento, the house was finished in Italian Stucco and filled with furniture purchased in Italy.[87]

Together, Arthur Little and Herbert Browne produced designs for public and private buildings that encompassed both the colonial revival and Italian Renaissance idioms. The firm catered to wealthy clients and built houses in both resorts and urban areas. Some of the projects were quite ostentatious, such as the colonial revival summer residence of Frederick E. Smith of Chicago (circa 1900) at Little's Point in Swampscott, Massachusetts—a kind Mount Vernon with gambrel roofs—or the Italianate Larz Anderson House (1902–05) in northwest Washington, D.C.[88] Classical antiquity, Italian Renaissance neoclassicism, and American Georgian and federal neoclassicism were not seen as mutually exclusive design alternatives; quite the opposite, Little & Browne understood these expressions as part of a connected classical history. Their exploration of the architectural heritage of northern New England was grounded in Little & Browne's belief in a continuity between the Old and New worlds, which transcended the manifest distances—geographic, historical, material—between the cultures.

—K.D.M.

Hamilton House, circa 1787

Renovation attributed to Arthur Little with Herbert Browne, 1899
South Berwick

HAMILTON HOUSE, overlooking a tributary of the Piscataqua River in South Berwick, is named after its first owner, the merchant Jonathan Hamilton. The building (designed by an unknown architect) was begun about 1787, and Hamilton owned it until his death in 1802. It subsequently went through a series of owners until Alpheus Goodwin purchased the house in 1839. Sixty years later, the Goodwin family sold the property, which included the house and 110 acres, to Emily (Mrs. George) Tyson and her stepdaughter Elizabeth (known as Elise) Tyson, later Vaughan. Wealthy members of Boston cultural and social circles, the Tysons were led to the Hamilton House by local author Sarah Orne Jewett, whose stories and novels, set in towns loosely modeled on Maine communities, had contributed to popular interest in the colonial period and its architecture. There is some evidence that the Tysons hired Arthur Little and Herbert Browne to renovate the house, but there is little documentation of what the work consisted.[89] What is clear, however, is that Little & Browne adapted the Hamilton House as a part-time residence with all the up-to-date features that such use required. Their renovation underscored the classical basis of the Georgian-style building.[90] The Tysons, Arthur Little, and Herbert Browne traveled in the same elite social circles and had mutual acquaintances. Evidently, their social connection led to the commission.

William Barry's 1928 description of the house written as part of an essay on "Old Houses in South Berwick" gives an account of the building as it appeared after its expansion and renovation by Little & Browne:

> One enters a wide and spacious hall, extending front to rear, beneath the stair landing overhead. The rear entrance, which is an ample doorway with andirons on either side of it and framed in pilasters and entablature, appears to be either a new work, or a restoration of former early carpentry.[91]

Hamilton House, South Berwick, circa 1787, with renovations and additions attributed to Little & Browne, circa 1899

Hamilton House, photographed by Elise Tyson Vaughan in 1903

Hamilton House, Garden Cottage, circa 1907, interior

The center hallway, creating an axis through the building and providing a place for the stairway, is one of the principal features of the Georgian plan type. A reproduction of the original "pillar-and-arch" wallpaper in the hallway emphasized the classical tradition of the design.[92]

Barry's report also provides a sense of how the Hamilton House functioned when it still had its colonial revival additions, which were subsequently demolished:

> On the West side are lofty and commodious parlors, front and rear, with imposing, if comparatively plain, work in chimney pieces, door, windows, and window seats. The door of the outside wall here gave into an inviting loggia attached to the house, and consisting of rustic arbor work and green vines.[93]

As Barry suggests, Little & Browne had effectively addressed one of the major drawbacks of early houses from the perspective of turn-of-the-century renovators: the absence of porches, terraces, and other spaces that accommodated the modern pursuit of a restorative contact with nature. The added service areas were topped by balustrades in keeping with the architectural character of the house and covered

Hamilton House

George Porter Fernald, Hamilton House, parlor murals, 1905–06

Elise Tyson Vaughan, "Looking East from House," photograph featuring the garden at Hamilton House, 1902

with lattice work. Entwined with plants, the lattice would have made the wings merge with the landscape and allowed the original part of the building to stand out.

Barry also commented on the Hamilton House murals, "executed in accomplished style with picture views of nearby historic dwellings."[94] The paintings were done in 1905 by George Porter Fernald (1869–1920), who often worked with Little & Browne, over wallpaper put up earlier by the Tysons. In the dining room, Fernald painted a landscape of Renaissance villas, gardens, grottos, and picturesque towns that recalled Sicily and southern Italy.[95] In the parlor, a series of historic houses from southern Maine and coastal New Hampshire covered the walls. Focusing on examples of eighteenth- and early nineteenth-century neoclassicism, Fernald's murals underscored the continuity between the European classical tradition and earlier American architecture. This was a connection that Jewett had made much earlier, in 1881, when she described her view of Hamilton House as being "like a glimpse of sunshiny, idle Italy."[96]

The association between the classicism of the Hamilton House and its European precedents was also made in the landscape that was developed around the building. The design of the gardens, in which Little & Browne may have had a hand,

Hamilton House (opposite) and Garden Cottage (above)

was based on the formal Italian tradition and incorporated neoclassical elements like arches, columns, and urns. William Barry described the site at length:

> Within the garden, on the elevated brow of the...steep river bank, was a segment-shaped or meandering pergola with vines. This formal landscape garden consisted of quite three enclosures, ornamented and separated by parterres of bright blooming phlox of pink or white. In the entering enclosures near the Mansion might be a sun dial upon a high white pedestal, as one sauntered on the flagged walk of natural-surfaced granite stones.... In the second enclosure could be viewed...a shed-like slatted arbor...and at one side was upon its column-like high support the white basin of a fountain. Traversing the last and extreme eastern enclosure...we find the rising grade before mentioned, and at its height...is yet another white shaft with elaborately modeled pine-apple atop it. This is the limit of the premises.
>
> On the river side of one of the garden enclosures is an old shed of the estate (now made over into an artist's lodge). The woodwork within is time-worn. It is a clear-story structure, and upon the hewn tie beams are one or two considerable ship models. Upon either side at the chimney end, and one story height above the fire-place are tiny galleries with balustrades.[97]

Barry draws attention to the classical elements that tied the landscape to the house. He certainly must have appreciated the Hamilton House because it embodied the elements of his own architectural style, developed from the 1860s onward. He penned this description of Hamilton House and its gardens near the end of his life, and left out any mention of Arthur Little's involvement. There is no indication that the association between the two men continued beyond the years when they had both worked for Peabody & Stearns, some fifty years earlier. Perhaps Barry did not know of Little & Browne's role in transforming Hamilton House, but he clearly appreciated their views of eighteenth-century landscapes and buildings, which were compatible with his own.

—K.D.M.

Hamilton House, Garden
Cottage, view toward river

Elizabeth Perkins House, York, circa 1730–50, with renovations and additions, 1898–1935

Elizabeth Perkins House

Mary Sowles Perkins and Elizabeth Bishop Perkins

Elizabeth Perkins House, circa 1730–50
With renovations and additions, 1898–1935
York

BETWEEN THE LATE SEVENTEENTH century and the 1920s, the house best known as the summer residence of Elizabeth Bishop Perkins of New York City went from a modest three-room structure on the banks of the York River to a rambling colonial revival homestead. Its twentieth-century transformation under the guidance of two of York's most energetic amateur historians—Elizabeth Perkins and her mother Mary Sowles Perkins—testifies to the growing passion among summer residents for both waterfront property and historical architecture. In many respects, their development of their property paralleled, on a more modest level, the treatment of the Hamilton House and its grounds by the Tysons, with whom the Perkinses were acquainted.

The first house on the site, called the Piggin House, was probably built by a ferryman named William Hilton, Jr. in 1686. His services must have been in high demand; without the ferry crossing, a long detour to the west would have been required to travel between York, on the north side of the river; and Kittery, Maine and Portsmouth, New Hampshire on the south side. A "piggin" is a small wooden box with an upright stave to serve as a handle—a form suggested by the original house, which was relatively small with a chimney at one end. The property was sold in 1712 to Samuel Sewall and Joseph Holt, a shoemaker and blacksmith, respectively. It seems that the Piggin House was still standing at that time and later incorporated into the existing building as the dining room. When Sewall and Holt divided the property, the latter received the lot with the Piggin House; Holt's son lived there, and, by 1732, he added to the building and constructed a wharf and warehouse. Holt's additions transformed the house into a two-story dwelling from which a one-story kitchen ell projected to the rear. The house was most likely

Elizabeth Perkins House, bedroom, added circa 1920

Elizabeth Perkins House, bedroom

Elizabeth Perkins House, parlor

Elizabeth Perkins House, dining room

owned by the Sewall family through most of the nineteenth century, before it was sold in the 1890s to T. E. Huidekoper of Worcester, Massachusetts. Mary Sowles Perkins and Elizabeth Bishop Perkins purchased the property from his heirs in 1898. Despite the fact that their respective husband and father, the Reverend Newton Perkins, was alive at the time of the purchase, his name was not on the deed, and in fact, he seems to have been relatively uninvolved in the transformation of the house that followed.

The Perkins women's first alteration to the house occurred soon after its acquisition when the roof of the one-story kitchen ell was raised to add a second floor. Other additions followed, continuing after the death of Reverend Perkins in 1916 and including new service areas at the rear of the house. These comprised

Elizabeth Perkins House, "Maple Parlor"   Elizabeth Perkins House, bedroom

spaces that were considered essential by wealthy summer residents of the time, such as a modern kitchen and servants' quarters. Despite their wish to live in a house with twentieth-century conveniences, all of the Perkinses' additions to and alterations of the building worked to enhance its historical character. An addition from around 1920, Elizabeth's second-story bedroom, contained wood paneling salvaged from an eighteenth-century house in nearby Cape Neddick. Between 1927 and 1933, the dining room—the old Piggin House attached to the later construction—was remodeled in a project that included ripping out the plaster ceiling to expose the heavy wood structure beneath—implying that the Perkinses were not immune to the twentieth-century mania for exposed beams considered to be so redolent of the colonial period. They also paid tribute to earlier neoclassicism on the south elevation of the servants' wing. There they, or their unknown architect, installed two Palladian windows in the double gable,

MARY SOWLES AND ELIZABETH BISHOP PERKINS

which light the attic level. The double gable was a popular element of suburban and resort architecture from the late-nineteenth century onward, appearing for example in the work of John Calvin Stevens.[98]

Despite the proximity of their house to the York River, the Perkins women do not appear to have spent much time relaxing on the beach, boating, or making use of the golf course that lay on the other side of the river. Instead, they spent their time in York immersed in the town's history, taking on major roles in local historical organizations. Mary Perkins, for example, held a costumed gala on the grounds of her house, almost immediately after she bought it, to support the preservation of York's famous Old Gaol. Elizabeth Perkins founded the Society for the Preservation of Historic Landmarks in York County, the organization to which she left the house upon her death.[99] Elizabeth Perkins wrote passionately about York's history for the yearly pageants she was famous for staging, as well as for various periodicals. In an unpublished manuscript called "The Codfish Ghost," Perkins self-consciously embroidered the history of her house, inventing a seventeenth-century inhabitant named Timothy who murdered his wife with a salted cod, the stench of which permeated the building for centuries.[100] If the whiff of history in the Perkins House was not quite that literal, it was nonetheless pervasive as a consequence of Mary Sowles and Elizabeth Bishop Perkins' enhancement of the building's character through both their architectural and historical projects.

—K.D.M.

153

William H. Dabney, Jr., Redcote cottage, York Harbor, circa 1880

William H. Dabney, Jr. OF BALL & DABNEY

WILLIAM H. DABNEY, JR. (1855–1897) was in the vanguard of the Boston colonial revival. He was born at Fayal in the Azores, where his father was American vice consul, and studied architecture at MIT between 1871 and 1875. The education he would have received there was modeled on the pedagogy of the Ecole des Beaux-arts. Its inherent historicism was complemented by the interest in early American architecture that was then growing in some Boston firms. During the second half of the 1870s, Dabney traveled abroad, worked as a draftsman for the Boston Water Works, and executed commissions for mills and other industrial buildings in New England. He married Marianne Parker, and the two spent some time living in the Azores before eventually settling in Brookline, Massachusetts.

Dabney is best known for an early barnlike cottage named Redcote, built on the York River for a relative, which was published in the *American Architect and Building News* in September 1882.[101] From the modest central volume, a shed-roofed block extends from one side recalling the lean-to extensions on early houses. The focal point of the facade is an over-scaled triangular pediment above the center window. Such references to both vernacular and high-style buildings of earlier periods would resurface in Dabney's other Maine works.

Early commissions were undertaken by Dabney alone, but by 1890 he had formed a partnership with Henry B. Ball (b. 1866), a younger architect from Portsmouth, New Hampshire who had also been educated at MIT. During the relatively short period of seven years that the two men were in partnership, they produced designs for private residences and public buildings in the colonial revival style, some of them located in Maine.[102]

Following Dabney's death at the age of forty-two, Ball & Dabney's firm continued on under different names and with a variety of partners. By the time of Dabney's death, he and Ball had already become associated with Henry C. Hayward. The firm continued to work in the colonial revival style, and focused on suburban residential building in the Boston area.[103] W. C. Allison's Bar Harbor cottage was designed by Dabney and Hayward (circa 1896–97).

—K.D.M.

The Sorrento Public Library, 1893
Sorrento

DATING TO THE time when William H. Dabney was in partnership with Henry B. Ball, the Sorrento Public Library was praised at the time of its completion as an "appropriate contribution to the beauty and growth of Sorrento."[104] The building complemented the grand development schemes of Frank Jones, another Portsmouth man, and Charles A. Sinclair of Boston. Known as the "King of the Alemakers," Jones invested in railroads and hotels in northern New England that supported the consumption of his brewery products.[105] At Sorrento, located on Waukeag Neck on Frenchman Bay, Jones and Sinclair built a summer community to compete with Bar Harbor just to the southeast; Ball & Dabney's neoclassical library contributed a suggestion of cultural sophistication to their resort project. Local history (or perhaps just rumor) maintains that Jones was forced to build the library, which is large in size relative to the small population of Sorrento, to atone for marital infidelity. Period sources, however, describe the library as "a gift from Mrs. Frank Jones."[106]

William H. Dabney, Jr., the Sorrento Public Library, Sorrento, 1893

Sorrento's development had begun in 1888 when the hundred-room Hotel Sorrento was built by the Frenchman Bay and Mount Desert Land and Water Company, the driving force behind which was Frank Jones. About the same time, streets were laid out for cottage lots, a wharf was constructed to enable steamboats to land summer visitors at Sorrento, and a fresh-water supply to the newly con-structed houses was established. In 1895 Sorrento was officially set off from the town of Sullivan of which it had been a part. When the Hotel Sorrento burned in the late spring of 1906, it was not replaced so that subsequent visitors had to rent or construct their own cottages.[107] Thus was established one of the defining char-acteristics of Sorrento, especially in comparison to other Maine coast resorts: it has no large hotels, and its summer life revolves around home owners, both year-round and seasonal.

The Sorrento Public Library

Although Sorrento never became as populous or renowned as Bar Harbor, it nonetheless gained its share of shingle-style cottages, whose designs are reflected in the library. The building, still serving its original function, has the encircling porch associated with summer residences and is covered by shingles, which were widely used for cottage siding along the New England coast. At the center of the interior is a dramatic two-story space surrounded by galleries, which allows the building to be a social center for the community. At the time of the library's com-pletion, the *Bar Harbor Record* wrote that "of course there are alcoves for books in every conceivable place, both below and in the galleries. The inside finishing is of native wood in natural colors with trimmings of ivory white."[108] The public func-tion of a library is emphasized by the library's neoclassical details, including the Palladian windows that figure prominently in the dormers. Ball & Dabney's design thus fit in with Sorrento's overall architectural character while its neoclassical ele-ments raised the building above the level of the surrounding cottages.

—K.D.M.

The Stackpole Block (attributed to William H. Dabney), 1894–95
York Harbor

EVERY SUMMER RESORT needs commercial space, and, despite its quiet gentility, York Harbor was no exception. Larger in scale, closer to the road, and more formal in its architecture than the rest of the buildings around the harbor, the Stackpole Block (now the Lancaster Building) is a unique work in its local context.

Frederick Dabney Stackpole, the architect's client, was likely a relative of Dabney's and certainly a booster of York Harbor. Not only did he commission several local buildings from Dabney, but he also wrote in glowing terms about the health benefits of summering in York Harbor. A physician from Roxbury, Massachusetts, Stackpole claimed of the resort in 1895 that "in my fifteen years of experience and practice here I have never known a case of serious illness to originate here."[109]

Although Stackpole's claim may have been somewhat exaggerated, it is true that at the end of the nineteenth century—when this building was constructed—

The Stackpole Block, attributed to William H. Dabney, Jr., York Harbor, 1894–95

158

York Harbor and other resorts along the New England coast were thought to offer healthful escapes from the scorching summer weather in cities to the south. Disease was believed to spread among crowded populations in urban settings. In addition, York was already, early in the nineteenth century, considered "old" since it had been an important port in the eighteenth century. Summer visitors came here not just for the beautiful coastal landscape, but also for the history of the place, represented in its clusters of eighteenth- and early nineteenth-century houses around the town's several villages.

Dabney's design of the Stackpole Block reinforced the historical character of the town while serving the practical needs of its visitors. The building housed stores for the boaters who docked at York Harbor and other summer residents, and included, at one point in its history, a movie theatre. With its neoclassical details, reminiscent of eighteenth-century buildings, the Stackpole Block recalled York's moment of greatest prosperity and importance. The two principal elevations both feature Palladian windows and are framed by pilasters. At the first story, quoins are used at the corners. The main facade on York Street has a central entrance that once accessed the movie theater; the side elevation possesses a series of entrances and Palladian shop windows.[110] ❧

—K.D.M.

The Stackpole Block

The Continuing Tradition
of the Colonial Revival in Maine

Frederick A. Tompson
The Richard Goodnow House

Joseph Dane and Fred C. Winslow
The Reverend Augustus M. Lord House

Frederick A. Tompson

AFTER HAVING APPRENTICED at the office of Portland architect Francis H. Fassett, Frederick A. Tompson (1857–1919) formed a partnership with his mentor in 1885. Among the buildings their firm designed in the expanding city was the three-story brick commercial block for merchant Asa Hanson, built in 1889 on Congress Street in the heart of the business district.[1] In 1891 Tompson opened his own firm and was responsible for the design of many civic and residential structures, including the Kotzschmar Hall, an opera house. Tompson is perhaps best known for his designs in the colonial revival style; the palatial house he designed for George C. West on the Western Promenade in Portland in 1911 provides a good example. The facade of the two-and-a-half-story building is dominated by the ionic columns that front the center entrance. At 12,000 square feet, the West House is believed to remain Portland's largest private residence.[2]

—K.D.M.

Frederick A. Tompson,
George C. West House,
Portland, 1911

The Charles Goodnow House, 1904
Kennebunk

THE GOODNOW HOUSE stands alongside some of Kennebunk's finest examples of the earlier architectural styles from which the colonial revival evolved. The house, with its large wrap-around porch and historicist detail, is reminiscent of summer cottages constructed at Kennebunk Beach and in Kennebunkport during the same period.

In 1903 Charles Goodnow, a wealthy Kennebunk businessman, purchased the original house on the site, the Joseph Hatch House (circa 1800), and hired Portland architect Frederick A. Tompson to build a more contemporary house. Tompson, who between 1898 and 1911 designed three imposingly large residences in Portland that employed classical and colonial elements,[3] would have been known to Goodnow as an architect capable of designing a house that fit in with the historic architecture of the surrounding area, while also conveying Goodnow's social standing.

Frederick A. Tompson, the Charles Goodnow House, Kennebunk, 1904

Charles Goodnow House

The surviving Hatch House on Goodnow's property was demolished, but Tompson's design for the new residence incorporated the basic elements of a colonial dwelling with a wealth of colonial revival detail. The massing of the Goodnow House is reminiscent of a colonial four-square with a center hallway, but the traditional gable roof has been replaced by a high hip roof with a large gabled dormer, which features a Palladian window on the front. Smaller gabled dormers with enclosed pediments are placed on each of the minor elevations, and a pair of large, asymmetrically placed chimneys pierce the roof. A partial roof balustrade follows the contours of the rounded bay on the right of the facade and terminates with urns on each end. Such classical elements are combined with other forms, such as bay windows and towers, that are more characteristic of the Queen Anne style.

The Goodnow House is one of Kennebunk's finest examples of the colonial revival style, designed by one of Maine's foremost turn-of-the-century architects. Tompson's abundant neoclassical details create an illusion of asymmetry, although the design is based on the symmetrical facades of the neighboring historic houses of Kennebunk's ship owners and merchants from the early Republic.

— R.M.

Joseph Dane

FROM 1935 UNTIL his death in 1963, Joseph Dane (1896–1963) was employed by, and subsequently became partner in, the architectural firm of Coolidge, Shepley, Bulfinch and Abbott.[4] Although Dane is not well known, he had a family connection to the Kennebunk area; indeed, the home he designed for Reverend Augustus Lord (in the years just prior to his joining the prestigious Boston firm) stands not far from Dane Street.

—R.M.

Reverend Augustus M. Lord House, 1933–34
Kennebunk

THE REVEREND AUGUSTUS Lord House was "built according to early colonial specifications" in 1933–34 as a summer home by a descendant of one of Kennebunk's founding families.[5] The colonial revival house and its parklike setting present a contemporary interpretation of the home's historic neighbors on Summer Street, blending seamlessly into a neighborhood that includes many late eighteenth- and nineteenth-century residences of ship captains and merchants. At the same time, the house pays homage to the ancestors of Reverend Lord's wife.

The original house on the site was constructed around 1800 by the attorney Joseph Dane. It burned in 1813, and the lot remained vacant until 1875 when it was purchased by Hartley Lord. Lord built a stable, which he moved three sites south in 1885, and sold the empty lot to his brother Robert W. Lord. In 1933 Robert Lord's daughter, Frances, and her husband, the Reverend Augustus M. Lord, purchased the property and constructed a summer home designed by architect Joseph Dane, a direct descendant of the owner of the original house on the lot.[6]

The design of the Augustus Lord House combines elements of both eighteenth- and nineteenth-century houses in the area. The most prominent feature on the five-bay main block is the oversized pedimented door surround. Stone steps lead up to the six-panel door, framed by a colonial surround incorporating Doric pilasters topped with a triangular pediment. The colonial revival interpretation of the doorway is revealed by the placement of a semicircular shuttered fanlight that extends

Joseph Dane, Augustus Lord House, Kennebunk, 1933–34

into the base of the tympanum. The hip roof, characteristic of Maine homes from the early Republic, has been heightened, and two symmetrically placed massive interior chimneys dominate the roofline.

The window openings are proportionately larger than those on earlier houses, indicating a modern preference for light-filled rooms. The dark green shutters set off against the stark white walls represent a common painting scheme used in New England villages, then thought to be consistent with colonial preferences. The large living room that occupies one half of the first story fulfills a twentieth-century desire for open living spaces.

The setting of the Lord House also shows how eighteenth- and nineteenth-century models were adapted in the twentieth century. When the present house was constructed, it was sited much further back on the lot than was the original house. This allowed for an expansive front lawn, which by the 1930s was deemed essential to a suburban or rural residence. The formality of the setting is enhanced by plantings at the foundation.

While the overall design of the Reverend Lord House evokes a romanticized ideal of an earlier era, its architectural details and landscaping bespeak a colonial revival home of the twentieth century. By the time of its construction, the colonial revival style had become among the most popular for suburban residences. ❧

—R.M.

Advertisement for the
Aluminum Window
Corporation, *House Beautiful*
89 (May 1947)

Colonial

designed for House & Garden by Robert C. Carr

A SMALL house, designed for a country site or the suburbs, this supplies a two-car garage, with maid's room, kitchen and pantry all in a wing under a long side roof. The front hall gives easy access to the living room and beyond that the dining room. For the man of the house there is reserved a bookroom directly at the end of the hall and opening at the farther end onto the terrace. The lord and master of this establishment can come and go with the least domestic interference. Upstairs are three bedrooms, two with connecting baths and the third served by a bath in the upper hall.

The rear terrace is a pleasant feature. From it one steps down to the garden or into the garage.

Of course, if this house is to follow Connecticut precedent, it will be painted white with bottle green blinds.

Robert C. Carr, "Colonial designed for House & Garden," *House & Garden* 70 (August 1936)

Notes

INTRODUCTION

1. See Margaret Henderson Floyd, "Measured Drawings of the Hancock House by John Hubbard Sturgis: A Legacy to the Colonial Revival," in *Architecture in Colonial Massachusetts: A Conference Held by the Colonial Society of Massachusetts, September 19 and 20, 1974* (Boston: The Colonial Society of Massachusetts, 1979).

2. Madelene Y. Wynne, "Time and Chance," *House Beautiful* VII (Jan. 1900): 72.

3. Overviews of the colonial revival movement can be found in William B. Rhoads, *The Colonial Revival* (New York and London: Garland Publishing, 1977); and Alan Axelrod, ed., *The Colonial Revival in America* (New York and London: W. W. Norton for the Henry Francis du Pont Winterthur Museum, 1985).

4. Quoted in the introduction to Henry Wadsworth Longfellow, *Tales of a Wayside Inn* (1863; repr., Cambridge, Mass.: Riverside Press, 1872), ix.

5. Quoted in Charles B. Hosmer, Jr., *The Presence of the Past: A History of the Preservation Movement in the United States before Williamsburg* (New York: G. P. Putnam's Sons, 1965), 281. Emphasis in the original.

6. Susan Larkin, *The Cos Cob Art Colony: Impressionists on the Connecticut Shore* (New York: National Academy of Design; New Haven: Yale University Press, 2001).

7. Keith N. Morgan, *Charles A. Platt: The Artist as Architect* (New York: The Architectural History Foundation; Cambridge, Mass. and London: MIT Press, 1985), 24.

8. This research is considered in greater depth in the essay "Picturesque and Refined: The Colonial Revival in Maine," in this volume.

9. Mary Caroline Crawford, *Romantic Days in the Early Republic* (New York: Grosset & Dunlap, 1912), 402.

10. In 1917 Mary Harrod Northend, the author of many books on colonial architecture and furnishings, could observe that "Architects of the present are coming to appreciate [the] worth [of colonial houses], and into many modern homes features of early construction are being incorporated." Mary H. Northend, *Colonial Homes and Their Furnishings* (Boston: Little, Brown, and Co., 1917), 14–15.

11. Dona Brown, "Purchasing the Past: Summer People and the Transformation of the Piscataqua Region in the Nineteenth Century," in *"A Noble and Dignified Stream": The Piscataqua Region in the Colonial Revival, 1860–1930,* ed. Sarah L. Giffen and Kevin D. Murphy (York, Maine: Old York Historical Society, 1992), 3–14.

12. Rick Nowell, "Capsule History of the Boston and Maine Railroad," Boston and Maine Railroad Historical Society Archives, http://www.trainweb.org/bmrrhs/history.html. The records of the Eastern Railroad Company of Massachusetts are held in the Baker Library Historical Collections, Harvard University, Cambridge, Mass.

13. Dona Brown, "Purchasing the Past," 6.

14. The point is substantiated by the use of colonial revival forms for such modern building types as the motel and the gas station. See William B. Rhoads, "Roadside Colonial: Early American Design for the Automobile Age," *Winterthur Portfolio* 21 (summer/autumn 1986): 133–52.

PICTURESQUE AND REFINED

1. R. S. Peabody, "The Georgian Houses of New England—II," *American Architect and Building News,* 18 February 1878, 54–55.

2. For more on the shingle style, see Vincent J. Scully, *The Shingle Style and the Stick Style,* rev. ed (New Haven and London: Yale University Press, 1971); and Leland M. Roth, *Shingle Styles, Innovation and Tradition in American Architecture 1874 to 1982* (New York: Harry N. Abrams, Inc., 1999).

3. Col. Russell H. Conwell, *History of the Great Fire in Boston, November 9 and 10, 1872* (Boston: B. B. Russell, 1873), 90.

4. Arthur Little, in the preface to his *Early New England Interiors* (Boston: A. Williams and Co., 1878), np.

5. Dona Brown, "Purchasing the Past," 3.

6. Ellis F. Lawrence, "John Calvin Stevens," *Architecture* 66 (July 1932): 2. Lawrence is here referring to the 1880s "when Stevens entered the profession."

7. William Pain published the influential *The Builder's Companion* in 1758. In later books, such as *The Practical Builder* (1774), Pain made the Roman-inspired style of English architect Robert Adam available to American builders in affordable books.

8. James Leo Garvin, "Academic Architecture and the Building Trades in the Piscataqua Region of New Hampshire and Maine, 1715–1815" (Ph.D. diss., Boston University, 1983), 296–97, 368–69.

9. On Eaton's projects in southern Maine, see Richard M. Candee, "'The Appearance of Enterprise and Improvement': Architecture and the Coastal Elite of Southern Maine," in *Agreeable Situations: Society, Commerce, and Art in Southern Maine, 1780–1830,* ed. Laura Fecych Sprague (Kennebunk, Maine: The Brick Store Museum, 1987), 75–79; and Arthur J. Gerrier, "Thomas Eaton," *Biographical Dictionary of Architects in Maine* 5 (Augusta and Portland, Maine: Maine Historic Preservation Commission and Maine Citizens for Historic Preservation, 1988).

10. The talk was later published in the *American Architect and Building News* and in two subsequent articles.

11. R. S. P[eabody], "A Talk about 'Queen Anne,'" *American Architect and Building News*, 28 April 1877, 133–34.

12. Ibid.

13. Georgian [pseud. of Robert Peabody], "Georgian Houses of New England," *American Architect and Building News*, 20 October 1877, 338.

14. Ibid., 339.

15. Peabody, "The Georgian Houses of New England—II," 54.

16. Ibid, 54–55. Peabody cites the second, 1811, edition of Asher Benjamin's *American Builder's Companion*.

17. Georgian, "Georgian Houses of New England," 338.

18. Ibid., 339.

19. Wheaton A. Holden, "The Peabody Touch: Peabody and Stearns of Boston, 1870–1917," *Journal of the Society of Architectural Historians* 32, no. 2 (May 1973): 122.

20. Wheaton Holden has called Peabody's Denny House "a pivotal house in the emergence of the American colonial revival and one that seems to have attracted the attention of William Ralph Emerson and Arthur Little among others." Ibid., 122.

21. Arthur Little, *Early New England Interiors* (Boston: A. Williams and Co., 1878). The image on the title page was also used on the cover of the book.

22. Little's alteration was drawn and published by Frank Wallis in *The American Architect and Building News*, and the original art work is held in the collection of the Society for the Preservation of New England Antiquities (S.P.N.E.A.), Boston, Mass. Bainbridge Bunting, *Houses of Boston's Back Bay: An Architectural History, 1840–1917* (Cambridge, Mass. and London: Belknap Press, 1967), 49–51; Mark Girourd, *Sweetness and Light: The Queen Anne Movement, 1860–1900* (New Haven and London: Yale University Press, 1977), 62–63.

23. "We made sketches and measured drawings of many of the important

colonial houses. . . . I think these drawings represent some of the earliest records of the colonial period, through native drawings. . . . I think the leaning of this office toward classic form dates from this trip." William Rutherford Mead, "Reminiscences," quoted in *McKim, Mead & White, Architects*, ed. Leland M. Roth, (New York: Harper & Row, 1983), 46.

24. See Richard Chaffee, "The Teaching of Architecture at the Ecole des Beaux-Arts" in *The Architecture of the Ecole des Beaux-Arts*, ed. Arthur Drexler (New York: Museum of Modern Art, 1977), 61–110.

25. Robert Peabody, quoted in an untitled and undated typescript by Wheaton Holden, Manuscript Division, Brown University Library, Providence, R.I.

26. Barry's early interest in historic buildings is demonstrated by drawings he made as a child. A large collection of Barry's personal papers from childhood onward survive in the Barry Collection [called Barry Family Papers in the Sources section], an archive established by his descendents and deposited in the Brick Store Museum, Kennebunk, Maine. Barry's sketchbooks are contained in pamphlet boxes 1 and 2, in Collection 29. An additional thirty-seven sheets of sketches and one sketchbook, mostly depicting historical architecture and furnishings, by William Barry are in the collection of the Maine Historical Society, Portland, Maine (collection cat. # O 1992.94).

27. For more on the Taylor-Barry House, see pages 74–79 of this volume.

28. On April 9, 1873, William Barry wrote to his brother Charles, "The portico is done and all say they like it." William E. Barry to Charles Barry, typescript, box #1, folder 15, Barry Collection, Brick Store Museum, Kennebunk, Maine. The originals of typescript letters are also in the Barry collection.

29. William Barry, *Pen Sketches of Old Houses* (Boston: James R. Osgood & Co., 1874).

30. Barry recorded his impressions in several sketchbooks, now held in the Brick Store Museum. For more on the plates in this book as well as its publication history, see the author's introduction to William E. Barry, *Pen Sketches of Old Houses* (1874; repr., Portland, Maine: Maine Preservation, 2002).

31. Of the latter, Barry wrote, "I do not think so much of that style of architecture for public buildings." William E. Barry to Sarah Perkins, 9 June 1872, typescript, box #1, folder 15, Barry Collection, Brick Store Museum.

32. William E. Barry to Sarah Perkins, 25 June 1872, typescript, box #1, folder 15, Barry Collection, Brick Store Museum.

33. The architect observed in Chester, England, "There were some buildings old and interesting enough, and much of the new that was built in the style of the old." William E. Barry to Sarah Perkins, 14 May 1872, typescript, box #1, folder 15, Barry Collection, Brick Store Museum.

34. William E. Barry to Sarah Cleaves Perkins, 29 August 1872, typescript, Barry Collection, Brick Store Museum.

35. Walter Knight Sturges has made the case for Barry's involvement in the Cliffs project on the basis of its similarity to Peabody's Denny House. As with the Denny House, the facades of the Cliffs are framed by giant pilasters. Similar skirting is used beneath the Palladian window on the Denny House and a pair of windows on the service wing of the Cliffs. There are also similarities between mantelpieces inside the two houses. See Walter Knight Sturges, "Arthur Little and the Colonial Revival," *Journal of the Society of Architectural Historians* XXXII (May 1973): 147–63.

The distinctive skirting that Sturges points to, which joins the sills of second-story windows to the lintels of first-story windows, is a recurring motif in Barry's sketches. In fact, the vertical layering of interconnected elements on a facade is an idea that is developed throughout his notebooks.

36. Sturges, "Arthur Little and the Colonial Revival," 150fn.

37. Dean T. Lahikainen, "Redefining Elegance: Benson's Studio Props," in *The Art of Frank W. Benson, American Impressionist*, exhib. cat. (Salem, Mass.: Peabody Essex Museum, 2000), 77–82.

38. Clarence Cook, *The House Beautiful* (1878; repr., Great Barrington, Mass.: North River Press, 1980), 147.

39. Edith Wharton and Ogden Codman, Jr., *The Decoration of Houses* (1902; repr., New York: W. W. Norton, 1978), 191.

40. The drawing is held in the S.P.N.E.A. Library and Archives. Wallis also published a neoclassical sofa owned by Little in his *Old Colonial Architecture and Furniture* (Boston and New York: Pollard & Co., 1887), np.

41. Ibid.

42. Frank E. Wallis, "What and Why is Colonial Architecture," *House and Garden* 16 (December 1909): 190–91.

43. Frank E. Wallis, *How to Know Architecture: The Human Elements in the Evolution of the Styles* (New York: Harper, 1910), 281.

44. Ibid.

45. John Calvin Stevens and Albert Winslow Cobb, *Examples of American Domestic Architecture* (1888: repr., Watkins Glen, N.Y.: The American Life Foundation & Study Institute, 1978), 12. See also the introduction to this volume by Earle G. Shettleworth, Jr. and William David Barry, np.

46. Ibid., 22–24.

47. Dona Brown, introduction to *A Tourist's New England: Travel Fiction, 1820–1920*, ed. Dona Brown (Hanover, N.H.: University Press of New England, 1999), 12.

48. Samuel Adams Drake, *Nooks and Corners of the New England Coast* (New York: Harper, 1875), quoted by Joyce Butler in a brochure published by the Brick Store Museum in conjunction with the exhibition, The Kennebunks: A Watering Place, the First Fifty Years, 1870–1920, July 1 through December 20, 1980. This brochure is the source of other information included here concerning the development of the Kennebunks as resorts. The plan for the subdivision of Lord's Point, book #2, plan #8, York County Registry of Deeds, Alfred, Maine.

49. For more on the Nathaniel Lord House, see pages 63–67 in this volume.

50. On the Samuel H. Jones Cottage (1887–88) and Rock Ledge, the E. Dunbar Lockwood Cottage (1887–88), see Roger G. Reed, *"A Delight to All Who Know It": The Maine Summer Architecture of William R. Emerson* (Augusta, Maine: Maine Historic Preservation Commission, 1990), 77–80, 82–83.

51. For more on the Colonel Harris House, see pages 80–85 in this volume.

52. For more on the Parson's Beach commissions, see pages 86–91 in this volume.

THE SENIOR DESIGNERS

1. Wheaton A. Holden, "The Peabody Touch: Peabody and Stearns of Boston, 1870–1917," *Journal of the Society of Architectural Historians* 32, no. 2 (May 1973), 114.

2. Ibid., 114fn.

3. The controversy surrounding the reorganization of the architectural section of the Ecole des Beaux-arts in 1863, and medievalist Eugène Emmanuel Viollet-le-Duc's role in it during his brief tenure as professor of the history of architecture, has been widely discussed. See, for example, M. F. Hearn, ed., *The Architectural Theory of Viollet-le-Duc* (Cambridge, Mass.: MIT Press, 1990), 9–10.

4. Robert S. Peabody to John D. Williams, 26 April 1868, typescript, Brown University Library, Providence, R.I.

5. Recollection of W. Cornell Appleton, a chief designer on Peabody's staff, quoted in Holden, "The Peabody Touch," 117.

6. Robert S. Peabody, "The Practice of Architecture in America," 7, typescript, Manuscript Division, Brown University Library.

7. Annie Robinson, "The Resort Architecture of Peabody & Stearns in Newport, Rhode Island, and Northeast Harbor, Maine" (M.A. thesis, Tufts University, Medford, Mass., 1999), 124–29.

8. *Industrial Journal*, 5 February 1897, quoted in Weston F. Milliken, "Peabody and Stearns," *A Biographical Dictionary of Architects in Maine* IV, no. 2 (Augusta, Maine: Maine Historic Preservation Commission, 1987).

9. Roger G. Reed, "Francis W. Chandler, 1844–1926," *A Biographical Dictionary of Architects in Maine* V, no. 4 (1988).

10. *Bangor Daily News*, 21 November 1913, quoted in Milliken, "Peabody and Stearns," [7].

11. Ibid.

12. Ibid.

13. Milliken, "Peabody and Stearns," [6].

14. Bainbridge Bunting, *Historic Houses of Boston's Back Bay: An Architectural History, 1840–1917* (Cambridge, Mass. and London: Belknap Press, 1967), 356.

15. For example, in 1859 Cabot designed a pair of houses at numbers 135 and 137 Beacon Street for the S. H. Russell and Charles Gibson families, who were related. Ibid., 155. The Gibson House is now operated as a museum.

16. Ibid., 231–35.

17. Richard Elia, "Edward Clarke Cabot, Watercolorist," *The Magazine Antiques* 114 (November 1978), 1068–69; Reed, "Francis W. Chandler."

18. The banquet proceedings are contained in a typescript in the vertical

files of the Rotch Library, Massachusetts Institute of Technology, Cambridge, Mass. A copy was kindly provided to me by Barbara E. Reed in 1985.

19. Historical background was provided by the Vinalhaven Historical Society, Vinalhaven, Maine. See also W. H. Bunting, comp. and annotator, *A Day's Work: A Sampler of Historic Maine Photographs, 1860–1920*, Part I (Gardiner and Portland, Maine: Tilbury House and Maine Preservation, 1997), 254–55.

20. Reed, "Francis W. Chandler".

21. Sarah Orne Jewett's letter was published in the Bangor *Industrial Journal*, 19 May 1893, 2. It is quoted in Earle G. Shettleworth, Jr., "Turn-of-the-Century Architecture: From about 1880 to 1920," in *Maine Forms of American Architecture*, ed. Deborah Thompson (Camden, Maine: DownEast Magazine, 1976), 197. Jewett is describing here something that sounds very much like her own family's house in South Berwick, Maine.

22. Reed, "Francis W. Chandler."

23. Booth Tarkington, *Mary's Neck* (Garden City, N.Y.: Doubleday, Doran, 1932), 2–3.

24. Roger G. Reed, "Francis W. Chandler."

25. The basic sources of information on Emerson's life are Cynthia Zaitzevsky, *The Architecture of William Ralph Emerson, 1833–1917*, exhib. cat. (Cambridge, Mass.: Fogg Art Museum, 1969); and Reed, *"A Delight to All Who Know It,"* esp. 11–12, from which the biographical information here is drawn.

26. Murray P. Corse, "The Old Ship Meeting-house in Hingham, Mass.," *Old-Time New England*, July 1930, 26.

27. Ibid.

28. William R. Emerson, "The Elimination of the Superfluous," *The Architectural Review*, November 1899, 142, quoted in Roger G. Reed, *"A Delight to All Who Know It,"* 20.

29. Arthur J. Gerrier, "Thomas Eaton," *A Biographical Dictionary of Architects* in *Maine* V. Blueprints of Emerson's drawings for the renovation of the house are held in the collection of the Kennebunkport Historical Society, Kennebunkport, Maine.

30. Wallis, "What and Why is Colonial Architecture?": 190.

31. This information derives from the New York, New Haven, and Hartford Railroad Archives, Thomas J. Dodd Research Center, University of Connecticut Libraries, Storrs, Conn.

Five years after Clark had the Lord Mansion enlarged, the railroad was taken over by J. P. Morgan and a group of investors from New York, and Charles Mellen was made president.

32. Harold Donaldson Eberlein and Donald Greene Tarpley, *Remodelling and Adapting the Small House* (Philadelphia: Lippincott, 1933), 19.

33. William Austin, "A History of the Boston Society of Architects," 1942, manuscript, Boston Athenaeum, Boston, Mass., quoted in Bunting, *Historic Houses of Boston's Back Bay*, 356.

34. Reed, *"A Delight to All Who Know It,"* 128–30.

THE DRAFTSMEN

1. William E. Barry to Sarah Perkins, Thursday, April 1864, typescript, William E. Barry Scrapbook, Barry Collection, Brick Store Museum. Emerson's mother, Olive Bourne Emerson, eventually remarried Captain Ivory Lord, who was William Barry's great-uncle.

2. William E. Barry to Sarah Perkins, Sunday, November 1864, typescript, William E. Barry Scrapbook, Barry Collection, Brick Store Museum.

3. Photographs of these drawings were later tipped into Barry's monograph, *The Blockhouse and Stockade Fort* (Kennebunk, Maine: Enterprise Press, 1915).

4. For his complete bibliography and a discussion of Barry as a historian, see Joyce Butler, introduction to *Sketch of an Old River*, by William E. Barry (1888; repr., Kennebunk, Maine: Brick Store Museum, 1993).

5. William E. Barry to William Lord, 9 July [1872], typescript, box #1, folder 15, Barry Collection, Brick Store Museum.

6. [Julia Bodman Barry], typescript note, William E. Barry Scrapbook, Barry Collection, Brick Store Museum. In the "Biographical Sketch of William E. Barry," *A Stroll Thro' the Past*, the authors write: "Upon his return to Kennebunk he continued his architectural work, and many of the buildings in this town and vicinity were designed by him. In this work he remained active until the time of his becoming incapacitated in 1931" (v–vi). Barry designed the 1906 renovation and expansion of the 1881 Cliff House.

7. A list of Barry's known commissions, documented by one account book of his work as an architect, is contained in Kevin Murphy, "William E. Barry, 1846–1932," *A Biographical Dictionary of Architects in Maine* I, no. 6 (Augusta, Maine: Maine Historic Preservation Commission, 1984).

8. The *Kennebunk Star* reported on December 22, 1882, "We are happy to learn that William E. Barry of Melrose, Mass., has purchased the Wallingford House and that he and his family will again become residents of this town." Barry had married Florence Wallingford Hooper on September 27, 1875.

9. Elise Lathrop, *Historic Homes of Early America* (New York: Tudor Publishing Co., 1927), 282–83. For a detailed history and description of the house, see Barba Architecture & Preservation in association with Kevin D. Murphy, "Taylor-Barry House, Kennebunk, Maine, Historic Structure Report," 2001, typescript, Taylor-Barry House files, Brick Store Museum.

10. William E. Barry to Sarah Perkins, August 1871, typescript, William E. Barry scrapbook, Barry Collection, Brick Store Museum.

11. Willam E. Barry to Charles Barry, 31 December 1972, typescript, book #1, folder #15, Barry Collection, Brick Store Museum.

12. On June 11, 1871, Sarah wrote to William, "The dining room will remain as it is until it has been painted, which it needs very much." On April 9, 1873, William Barry wrote to his brother, "We have decided to have the sitting room papered and I am going into Portland today to get the paper." Sarah Perkins to William E. Barry, [1871], Barry Collection, Brick Store Museum and William E. Barry to Charles Barry, 9 April 1873, typescript, box #1, folder 15, Barry Collection, Brick Store Museum.

13. Sarah Perkins to William E. Barry, [1871].

14. William E. Barry to Charles Barry, 9 April 1873.

15. William E. Barry to Jott S. Perkins, Sunday, October, 1871, typescript, box #1, folder 15, Barry Collection, Brick Store Museum.

16. Edward E. Bourne III and Hartley Lord II, *Kennebunk in the Nineties, and Biographical Sketches* (Kennebunk, Maine: Brick Store Museum, 1965), 67. I am also grateful to Mrs. James S. Coburn for her assistance in researching the history of the house.

17. In the summer of 1888, a nearby shingle-style cottage was built for W. A. Coleman of New York from Barry's plans. The local newspaper reported in July of that year, "Mr. Coleman's cottage is rapidly nearing completion. Mr. William Barry of Kennebunk Village is the architect and Mr. Joseph Day the builder. The work does these artists great credit." *The Wave*, 28 July 1888, 3.

18. The history of the house was compiled by Sandra S. Armentrout in connection with the 1982 William E. Barry exhibition and is part of the archival record of that project at the Brick Store Museum.

19. Booth Tarkington, *Mirthful Haven* (Garden City, N.Y.: Doubleday, 1930), 2–3.

20. William E. Barry exhibition materials, 1982, Brick Store Museum.

21. *The Wave*, 29 August 1888, 3. The history of the Parsons family houses is recorded in a series of commemorative plates of "family homes," produced around 1941. Copies are held in the collection of the Brick Store Museum. Barry's involvement at Parsons Beach is documented in his list of commissions.

22. "Parsons, Charles," in *The National Cyclopaedia of American Biography* IV (New York: James T. White & Co., 1897), 175.

23. Parsons family tradition maintains that Barry designed the White House/Tennis Court House. See the Kennebunk Beach Historic Building/Structure Survey Form for this house and other Parsons Beach commissions, Maine Historic Preservation Commission, Augusta, Maine.

24. William E. Barry to Sarah Lord Barry Perkins, January 1869, Barry Collection, Brick Store Museum; quoted in Sandra S. Armentrout and Joyce Butler, "Notes: William Barry letters to his family in Kennebunk," typescript, William E. Barry, exhibition materials, 1982, Brick Store Museum.

25. Hampden Fairfield, Esq., "Address of Presentation," in *The Dedication of the Charles C. G. Thornton Library Building at Thornton Academy, Feb. 28, 1903* (Saco, Maine: Charles C. G. Thornton Library, 1903), 3–5, 16.

26. No longer used as the library, it is now known as the Charles Thornton Memorial Building.

27. "Thornton Academy Library Building," clipping from an unknown source, 26 November 1902, Thornton Academy Archives, Saco, Maine.

28. Thomas Hardiman, National Register of Historic Places Nomination for a Portion of Main Street, Saco, Maine, 1996, Maine Historic Preservation Commission.

29. Kirk F. Mohney, *Beautiful in All Its Details: The Architecture of Maine's Public Library Buildings, 1878–1942* (Portland, Maine: Maine Preservation, 1997), 31.

30. Clifford Edward Clark, Jr., *The American Family Home, 1800–1960* (Chapel Hill and London: University of North Carolina Press, 1986), 62.

31. Gwendolyn Wright, *Building the Dream: A Society History of Housing in America* (Cambridge, Mass. and London: MIT Press, 1981), 112.

32. A typescript copy of this account, without a source but likely from a contemporary newspaper, is held in the Thornton Academy Archives.

33. Earle G. Shettleworth, Jr. and William David Barry, introduction to *Examples of American Domestic Architecture*, by John Calvin Stevens and Albert Winslow Cobb (1889; repr., Watkins Glen, N.Y.: The American Life Foundation, 1978), np.

34. Earle G. Shettleworth, Jr., "Turn-of-the-Century Architecture: From about 1880 to 1920," in *Maine Forms of American Architecture*, ed. Deborah Thompson (Camden, Maine: DownEast Magazine, 1976), 185–205.

35. Stevens and Cobb, *Examples of American Domestic Architecture*, np.

36. Ibid.

37. These lots were typically sold with restrictions imposing a five-foot setback on houses from adjoining lot lines and a fifteen-foot setback from the street. Any building erected had to be a dwelling house or private stable, and no house could be built costing less than $500. Thus the corporation established minimal controls on the nature of the development. The cost of the Deering House, at $8,500, was well over the threshold established by the deed restrictions.

38. *Industrial Journal*, 22 June 1888; *Scientific American, Building Edition*, November 1896, 88. In addition to the sketches for the house, there are plans and elevations (undated) for both the house and stable in the John Calvin Stevens Collection, Maine Historical Society, Portland, Maine.

39. In an 1890 review of the book for *The British Architect*, the same plate was featured among a sampling of illustrations.

40. Portland Society of Art, Seventeenth Exhibition, May 1888, *Building* (London), vol. 9, no. 24 (Dec. 15, 1888). *The British Architect*, January 24, 1890, 60.

41. It was the published design that is presumed to have influenced the house of A. J. Ward by C. F. A. Voysey, a drawing for which was published in the April 11, 1890 issue of *The British Architect*. See James D. Kornwolf, *M. H. Baillie Scott and the Arts and Crafts Movement* (Baltimore and London: The Johns Hopkins University Press, 1972), 66–68.

42. The cottage was sold to Julian Kaufman of New York two years before Deering's death. *Portland Board of Trade Journal*, May 1894, 7; *Portland Daily Press*, 27 April 1904.

43. *Industrial Journal*, 26 September 1890 and 14 November 1890.

44. Plans do not survive for the project, but two elevations for fireplace mantels exist in the John Calvin Stevens Collection. There are also handwritten specifications for the Brazier Cottage by Stevens. In 1904 Mrs. Brazier hired Stevens, then in partnership with his son, John Howard Stevens, to make minor changes to the house. In particular, a bathroom was added by building a small room with exterior shingles on the roof of the porte cochere. John Calvin Stevens to Mrs. Ellen K. Brazier, 16 June 1904, John Calvin Stevens Collection, Maine Historical Society.

45. Drawing entitled "House at South Manchester, Connecticut, John Calvin Stevens, Architect"; Robert Cheney to John Calvin Stevens, 6 November 1896; both held in the Stevens Collection, Maine Historical Society.

46. *Industrial Journal*, 26 September 1890 and 14 November 1890.

47. The drawings include a perspective study for a smaller house without an ell. A sketch plan for the first floor with the architect's notes of instructions from the client regarding room arrangements and interior finishes also survives. All are held in the John Calvin Stevens Collection, Maine Historical Society.

48. It appears from the drawings that the original porch columns for the verandah were Tuscan instead of the square posts that exist today. Only the small second-floor porch retains its original columns.

49. Book 453, 197–99, York County Registry of Deeds, Alfred, Maine; Book 458, 398–400, York County Registry of Deeds; E. H. Bronson to John Calvin Stevens, 7 September 1895, John Calvin Stevens Collection, Maine Historical Society.

50. "Brooklynites and their Summer Homes," *Brooklyn Eagle*, 8 July 1900, 35.

51. Book 477, 196–98, York Country Registry of Deeds; Book 487, 186–89, York Country Registry of Deeds.

52. John Calvin Stevens, drawing for Endcliffe, summer residence of F. W. Moss, Avery Library, Columbia University, New York, New York.

53. The chronology is indicated by book 487, 349–52, York County Registry of Deeds.

54. Earle G. Shettleworth, Jr., and John Calvin Stevens II, *John Calvin Stevens: Domestic Architecture, 1890–1930* (Scarborough, Maine: Harp Publications, 1990), 208.

55. Stevens and Cobb, *Examples of American Domestic Architecture*, np.

56. Kerry A. O'Brien, "Layers of Time: John Calvin Stevens, the Colonial Revival, and the York Institute" (unpublished paper, University of Southern Maine, 1989). This paper contains an extensive bibliography on source material for the York Institute building. Coverage of the York Institute was contained in the *Biddeford Daily Journal*, 4 December 1926, *Lewiston Journal, Illustrated Magazine Section*, 9 July 1927, and the *Lewiston Sun*, 8 October 1930.

57. O'Brien, "Layers of Time," 19.

58. "A Design for the Massachusetts Headquarters of the Exhibition in Philadelphia" by Henry Paston Clark was published in *The Architectural Sketchbook* vol. IV, no. V (Nov. 1876). The architect's father, Dr. Henry Grafton Clark, was an honorary member of the Massachusetts State Centennial Board and was involved in celebrations in Lexington in 1875. Henry Paston Clark, "Descendants of Rev. Jonas Clark," pp. 21, 29; typescript, collection of Ann Elmquist.

59. Letter to the author from Professor Richard Chafee, 12 October 1982, in which he referenced a listing of Clark as a student in the *American Architect* XXII, no. 610 (3 September 1887): 114.

60. Local newspaper reference, 1 March 1878, in notebook of Adelaide Day, Kennebunkport Historical Society, Kennebunkport, Maine. The Kennebunkport Post Office was built on the site after the hotel was demolished in the 1930s. Joyce Butler, *A Kennebunkport Album* (Kennebunk Landing, Maine: Rosemary House Press, 1984).

61. The Ocean Bluff, built in 1873, exemplifies the more informal style. It burned in 1898 and was not replaced until Breakwater Court (now the Colony) was built on its site in 1914. Joyce Butler, *Kennebunkport Scrapbook* I (Kennebunk, Maine: Thomas Murphy, 1977), 53.

62. One work by Vaughan & Clark— the Lower School at St. Paul's School, in Concord, New Hampshire, of 1891—is included in William Morgan, *Henry Vaughan: The Almighty Wall* (New York: Architectural History Foundation, and Cambridge, Mass.:

MIT Press, c1983). Morgan situates the Lower School as "the initiator of Vaughan's Georgian and institutional buildings" (124).

63. The Sprague Cottage was published in *American Architect and Building News*, 4 November 1882.

64. Photos and plans appeared in *Scientific American, Building Edition* 20 (July 1895).

65. *Scientific American, Building Edition* 19 (January 1895): 6–7.

66. Ibid, 7.

67. Kevin Gardner, "The Amoskeag Mills," New Hampshire Public Radio, June 3, 2002, http://nhpr.org/view_content/3205/.

68. "Manning, Charles Henry," in *Who Was Who in America* I (Chicago: A. N. Marquis Co., 1942), 774.

69. Mrs. Paul Elmquist, interview with the author, 24 September 1984.

70. A clipping of the obituary "Henry Paston Clark," possibly from a Kennebunk or Kennebunkport newspaper and held in the collection of Ann Elmquist, states, "Mr. Clark left a monument to his life in St. Ann's Episcopal Church. He was instrumental in its founding four decades go, was its designer, ministered to its growth stone by stone and week by week, to its present completion." St. Ann's is also the one building of Clark's mentioned in the obituary "Boston Architect Dead," *Boston Transcript*, 6 September 1927.

71. Description from the *Boston Sunday Herald* (1890), reprinted in *The Wave*, 12 July 1890.

72. Clark's other Episcopal churches, including St. George's in Sanford, Maine and St. Andrews-by-the-Sea in Hyannisport, Massachusetts, possessed crenellation and half-timbering.

73. Advertisement in the brochure "Kennebunkport and Kennebunk Beach, Maine" (New York: Geo. W. Richardson, undated), Brick Store Museum.

74. Clark's father had had his photograph taken there during the Civil War.

75. Henry Paston Clark, "Descendants of Rev. Jonas Clark," manuscript, collection of Ann Elmquist, 1.

76. Clark's finest works are an episode in the American rural "synthesis with nature." As such they belong in an architectural tradition somewhere between H. H. Richardson's Ames Gate Lodge, North Easton, Massachusetts, of 1881–82 and Frank Lloyd Wright's Fallingwater, Bear Run, Pennsylvania, of 1936–37.

77. Undated clipping from an Atlantic Shoreline Railway promotional brochure, Kennebunkport Historical Society.

78. Ibid.

79. Arthur Little, *Early New England Interiors* (Boston: A. Williams & Co., 1878).

80. For information on these projects, see Walter Knight Sturges, "Arthur Little and the Colonial Revival," *Journal of the Society of Architectural Historians* 32, no. 2 (May 1973): 147–63.

81. Richard Herndon and Edwin Bacon, comps., *Boston of To-day: A Glance at Its History and Characteristics* (Boston: Post Publishing Co., 1892), 294.

82. Bainbridge Bunting, *Historic Houses of Boston's Back Bay: An Architectural History, 1840–1917* (Cambridge, Mass. and London: Belknap Press, 1967), 330.

83. Harold Kirker, *The Architecture of Charles Bulfinch* (Cambridge, Mass.: Harvard University Press, 1969), 135–40.

84. I am grateful to J. R. Burrows & Co. for the identification of the fabrics. See also Catherine Lynn, "Surface Ornament: Wallpapers, Carpets, Textiles, and Embroidery," in *In Pursuit of Beauty: Americans and the Aesthetic Movement*, ed. Doreen Bolger Burke et al. (New York: Metropolitan Museum of Art, in collaboration with Rizzoli International, 1986), 71.

85. Little used this term in his correspondence only once, as far as the author knows, when he wrote to Codman with regard to a Mrs. or Miss Fisk that "I feel as if she must hold the position of *Virgin Mary to the Colonial Trinity!!!*" Arthur Little to Ogden Codman, Jr., 3 March 1892, Codman Papers, Society for the Preservation of New England Antiquities (S.P.N.E.A.) Library and Archives, Boston, Massachusetts. See also Christopher Monkhouse, "The Making of a Colonial Revival Architect," in Pauline c. Metcalf, ed., *Ogden Codman and the Decoration of Houses* (Boston: Boston Athenaeum and David R. Godine, 1988).

86. Arthur Little to Ogden Codman, Jr., 15 February 1892, typescript, Codman Papers, S.P.N.E.A. Library and Archives.

87. Information about the house was provided to the author by Nancy Hallowell in personal correspondence, 20 January 1985.

88. "A Successful Country House Designed by Arthur Little," *Ladies Home Journal* 18 (May 1900): 20; Society of the Cincinnati, *The Larz Anderson House in Washington* (Boston: Merrymount Press, 1938). Little purchased property in Bar Harbor, Maine, in 1889 with the intention of building a house for himself but never did so. He sold the land some time after 1903 to the adjoining homeowner, architect Fred L. Savage. Roger G. Reed, Personal correspondence to the author, 30 December 1985.

89. Little and Browne's account book, held in the S.P.N.E.A. Library and Archives, refers only to "Alterations to House at So. Berwick, Maine. 1899." Richard C. Nylander, "Hamilton House," in *A Noble and Dignified Stream*," ed. Giffen and Murphy, 71.

90. The renovation of Hamilton House is documented in *"A Noble and Dignified Stream,"* ed. Griffen and Murphy, 70–78, 97–104,

91. William E. Barry, "Old Houses in South Berwick (Visited and Described

by William E. Barry in 1928)," type-script, Barry Collection, Brick Store Museum.

92. Richard C. Nylander, Elizabeth Redmond, and Penny J. Sander, *Wallpaper in New England* (Boston: S.P.N.E.A., 1986), 268–69.

93. Barry, "Old Houses in South Berwick," Brick Store Museum.

94. Ibid.

95. Sandra S. Armentrout, "Hamilton House Murals," in "*A Noble and Dignified Stream*," ed. Giffen and Murphy, 76.

96. Sarah Orne Jewett, "River Driftwood," in *Country By-Ways* (Boston, Houghton, Mifflin and Company, 1881), quoted in Armentrout, "Hamilton House Murals," 74.

97. Barry, "Old Houses in South Berwick," Brick Store Museum.

98. Turk, Tracey & Larry Architects, "Historic Structure Report for Elizabeth Perkins House, Old York Historical Society, York, Maine," 16 February 2000, typescript, Old York Historical Society, York, Maine.

99. In 1984 Historic Landmarks merged with two other local historical organizations to become the Old York Historical Society, which now operates the Elizabeth Perkins House as a museum.

100. Elizabeth Bishop Perkins, "The Codfish Ghost: The Biography of a House from the Seventeenth Century to the Present Day," 1933, manuscript, Old York Historical Society.

101. Scully, *The Shingle Style and the Stick Style*, 89–90.

102. For further information on Dabney, see the author's entry "William H. Dabney, Jr., 1855–1897," in *A Biographical Dictionary of Architects in Maine* VI, and "William H. Dabney, Jr. (1855–97), Architect," in "*A Noble and Dignified Stream*," ed. Giffen and Murphy, 147–48.

103. Murphy, "William H. Dabney, Jr."

104. *Bar Harbor Record*, 13 July 1893.

105. On Jones, see Richard M. Candee, "Rockingham Hotel [and] Wentworth Hotel," in "*A Noble and Dignified Stream*," ed. Giffen and Murphy, 17.

106. *Bar Harbor Record*, 13 July 1893. Earle G. Shettleworth kindly brought this reference to my attention.

107. Mark Honey, "Sorrento's Grand Beginnings—As Sullivan," *Ellsworth American*, www.ellsworthamerican.com/our-town/sorrento/ot_sorren-to2_10-17-02.html.

108. *Bar Harbor Record*, 13 July 1893.

109. Frederick D. Stackpole, "York as a Health Resort," in *Health Resorts of the South and Summer Resorts of New England* (Boston: George H. Chapin Co., 1895), 335.

110. The interior was substantially altered when the building was converted to residential condominiums in the 1980s.

THE CONTINUING TRADITION

1. *Greater Portland Landmarks Observer* 26, no. 4 (winter 2001–2002): 1.

2. Clemmer Mayhew III, "Building Matters: Big Houses," *Casco Bay Weekly* 15, no. 10 (20 March 2003): 14.

3. Information on these commissions can be found on the Greater Portland Landmarks "Virtual Tour of the Western Promenade," http://www.portlandlandmarks.org/go_western_promenade_tour.htm#1.

4. In 1952 the firm's name changed to Shepley, Bullfinch, Richardson and Abbott.

5. An undated newspaper article lists Fred C. Winslow as the house's builder, *Summer Street* binders, the Brick Store Museum, Kennebunk, Maine. For information on this and adjacent houses, see Rosalind Magnuson, *An Architectural Walking Tour of Kennebunk's National Register Historic District* (Kennebunk, Maine: Brick Store Museum, 1993).

6. George A. Gilpatric, *Kennebunk History: Not a History of Kennebunk but a Few Items in Addition to and a Sequel to "The Village of Kennebunk, Maine"* (Kennebunk, Maine: Star, 1939), 29–30.

Selected Sources on the Colonial Revival in Maine

PRINCIPAL ARCHIVAL HOLDINGS

Barry Collection, Brick Store Museum, Kennebunk, Maine

Historic American Buildings Survey Collection, Library of Congress, Washington, D.C.

John Calvin Stevens Collection, Maine Historical Society, Portland, Maine

Little & Browne Papers, Society for the Preservation of New England Antiquities, Boston, Mass.

Peabody & Stearns Collection, Boston Public Library, Boston, Mass.

PERIOD LITERATURE

Barry, William E. *The Blockhouse and Stockade Fort: A Monograph.* Kennebunk, Maine: Enterprise Press, 1915.

———. *Pen Sketches of Old Houses.* Boston: James Osgood, [1874].

———. *A stroll thro' the past, accompanied by an invisible associate, and using an 18th century stage-route and river ford, preceded by a summary of the early ownerships and provincial governments of Maine, together with a collection of historical data gathered in and around Kennebunk Village and sketches of buildings which have long since disappeared.* Portland, Maine: Southworth Press, 1933.

Chandler, Joseph Everett. *The Colonial House.* New York: R. M. McBride & Co., 1916.

Corner, James W. and E. E. Soderholtz. *Examples of Domestic Architecture in New England.* Boston: Boston Architectural Club, 1892.

Fiske, John. *The Beginnings of New England: Or, the Puritan Theocracy in its Relation to Civil and Religious Liberty.* Boston: Houghton, Mifflin and Co., 1889.

Howells, John Mead. *The Architectural Heritage of the Piscataqua: Houses and Gardens of the Portsmouth District of Maine and New Hampshire.* New York: Architectural Book Publishing Company, Inc., 1937.

———. *Lost Examples of Colonial Architecture.* Boston[?]: William Helburn, 1931.

Kimball, Fiske. *Domestic Architecture of the American Colonies and the Early Republic.* New York: Metropolitan Museum of Art, 1922.

Lamb, Martha J., ed. *The Homes of America.* New York: D. Appleton and Company, 1879.

Little, Arthur. *Early New England Interiors.* Boston: A. Williams and Co., 1878.

Nason, Emma Huntington. *Old Colonial Houses in Maine Built prior to 1776.* Augusta, Maine: Kennebec Journal, 1908.

Nutting, Wallace. *Maine Beautiful: A Pictorial Record Covering all the Counties of Maine with Text Between.* Framingham, Mass.: Old America Co., 1924.

Porter, Frederick Hutchinson. "A Survey of Existing Colonial Architecture in Maine." *Architectural Review* 7 (1918).

Walker, C. Howard. *An Architectural Monograph on Some Old Houses of the South Coast of Maine.* St. Paul, Minn.: White Pine Bureau, 1918.

Wallis, Frank E. *Old Colonial Architecture and Furniture.* Boston: George H. Polley & Co., 1887.

Ware, William Rotch. *The Georgian Period: A Collection of Papers Dealing with "Colonial" or XVIII-Century Architecture in the United States.* 4 vols. Boston: American Architect and Building News Company, 1898–1902.

Whitefield, Edwin. *The Homes of Our Forefathers, Being a Selection of the Oldest and Most Interesting Buildings, Historical Houses, and Noted Places in Maine, New Hampshire, and Vermont, from Original Drawings Made on the Spot.* Reading, Mass.: E. Whitefield, 1886.

SECONDARY LITERATURE

Brown, Dona. *Inventing New England*. Washington, D.C.: Smithsonian Institution Press, 1997.

Conforti, Joseph. *Imagining New England: Exploration of Regional Identity from the Pilgrims to the Mid-Twentieth Century*. Chapel Hill, N.C.: University of North Carolina Press, 2001.

Giffen, Sarah, and Kevin D. Murphy, eds. *"A Noble and Dignified Stream": The Piscataqua Region in the Colonial Revival, 1860–1930*. York, Maine: Old York Historical Society, 1992.

Gyure, Dale Allen, and Karen Mulder. *Colonial Revival in America: Annotated Bibliography*. 2003 Web edition, http://etext.lib.virginia.edu/colonial/.

Holden, Wheaton. "The Peabody Touch: Peabody and Stearns of Boston, 1870–1917." *Journal of the Society of Architectural Historians* XXXII (May 1973): 114–31.

Murphy, Kevin D. "William E. Barry (1846–1932)." In *Biographical Dictionary of Architects in Maine*, vol. I. Augusta, Maine: Maine Historic Preservation Commission, 1984.

———. "'A Stroll Thro' the Past': Three Architects of the Colonial Revival." Master's thesis, Boston University, 1985.

Reed, Roger G. *"A Delight to All Who Know It": The Maine Summer Architecture of William R. Emerson*. Augusta, Maine: Maine Historic Preservation Commission, 1990.

Rhoads, William B. *The Colonial Revival*. New York: Garland Publishing, 1977.

———. "The Discovery of America's Architectural Past, 1874–1914." In *The Architectural Historian in America*. Edited by Elisabeth Blair MacDougall. Washington, D.C.: National Gallery of Art, 1990.

Scully, Vincent J. *The Shingle Style and the Stick Style*. New Haven, Conn.: Yale University Press, 1955.

Shettleworth, Earle G., and John Calvin Stevens II. *John Calvin Stevens: Domestic Architecture, 1890–1930*. Scarborough, Maine: Harp, 1990.

Sprague, Laura Fecych, ed. *Agreeable Situations: Society, Culture, and Art in Southern Maine, 1780–1830*. Kennebunk, Maine: The Brick Store Museum, 1987.

Sturges, Walter Knight. "Arthur Little and the Colonial Revival." *Journal of the Society of Architectural Historians* XXXII (May 1973): 147–63.

Thompson, Deborah, ed. *Maine Forms of American Architecture*. Camden, Maine: DownEast Magazine, 1976.

Truettner, William H., and Roger B. Stein, eds. *Picturing Old New England*. New Haven: Yale University Press, 1999.

Wilson, Richard Guy. *The Colonial Revival House in America*. New York: Abrams, 2004.

Wilson, Richard Guy, and Sidney K. Robinson, eds. *Modern Architecture in America: Visions and Revisions*. Ames, Iowa: Iowa State University Press, 1991.

Zaitzevsky, Cynthia. *The Architecture of William Ralph Emerson, 1833–1917*. Cambridge, Mass.: Fogg Art Museum, 1969.

Illustration Credits

American Architect and Building News: (16 Feb. 1878), courtesy of the Athenaeum of Philadelphia, p. 20; (6 July 1878), courtesy of the Avery Architectural and Fine Arts Library, Columbia University, p. 23; (26 Nov. 1881), courtesy of the Avery Architectural and Fine Arts Library, Columbia University, p. 12; *American Architect and Building News* (1882), courtesy of the Society for the Preservation of New England Antiquities, p. 154

Architecture 66 (July 1932), p. 15

Bednarek, Nicola, pp. 131 top, 134, 148 top and bottom, 158, 159, 164, 166

Benjamin, Asher, *The Country Builder's Assistant* (Boston: Spotswood and Etheridge, 1798), courtesy of the Pocumtuck Valley Memorial Association, Deerfield, Mass., p. 17

Boston Public Library, p. 48

Brick Store Museum: pp. iv, 23, 24, 25, 26, 28 bottom, 38, 65, 71, 73 top, 75, 76, 77, 165; photograph by Sandra Armentrout, pp. 90, 91; photograph by David Bohl, pp. ii, 37, 63, 79, 80, 84, 92, 114, 132; photograph by Victor N. Camp ca. 1939, p. 70; ca. 1870, p. 78; ca. 1890, pp. 41 bottom, 83; ca. 1900, pp. 41 top, 74, 86, 128; ca. 1910, p. 94; ca. 1915, pp. 160–61, 163; ca. 1920, p. 133; ca. 1950, p. 89

Cambridge Historical Commission, ca. 1893, p. 136 right

Dennis, Robert A., p. 131

Florence Griswold Museum, p. 64

Hanser, David A., p. 22

Hopkins, Eric, pp. 56, 59

House & Garden (Aug. 1936), p. 167 left

House Beautiful (May 1947), p. 167 right

Kennebunkport Historical Society, p. 66 top and bottom; ca. 1890, p. 123

Library of Congress Prints and Photographs Division: PAN US GEOG—Maine, no. 5, p. 129; HABS, MASS,13–BOST,104–1, SPNEA Collection, p. 1; HABS, ME,16–BERN.V,1–6, photograph by Frank D. Sampson, 1936, p. x; HABS, ME,16–KEN,1–4, p. 9

Little, Arthur, *Early New England Interiors* (Boston: A. Williams & Co., 1878), p. 21

Lovejoy, Kim, p. 135

Maine Historic Preservation Commission: pp. 14, 87 top and bottom, 111 top; photograph by Kim Lovejoy, pp. 106, 108, 109; photograph by Kevin Murphy, pp. 81, 90 left; ca. 1890, p. 58; ca. 1900, p. 55; ca. 1930, p. 119

Maine Historical Society, pp. 101 left and right, 107, 110

Maine Publicity Bureau *News* (Nov.–Dec. ca. 1955), courtesy of the Maine Historical Society, p. 34

Mayhew III, Clemmer, pp. 44–45, 49, 51 top, bottom left, and bottom right, 162

McArthur Library, Biddeford, Maine, p. 95 top

Murphy, Kevin, pp. 22 top, 52–53, 95 bottom, 124, 125, 156, 157

Old York Historical Society: pp. 3, 150 top, bottom left, and bottom right, 152 left and right; photograph by Douglas Armsden, ca. 1953, p. 151

Old-Time New England (July 1930), p. 61 top and bottom

Palladio, Andrea, *The Four Books of Architecture* (1570), p. 17

Private Collection, p. 130; p. 137 bottom; ca. 1890, p. 129; ca. 1900, p. 122; ca. 1910, p. 73

Scientific American Building Edition: (Jan. 1895), courtesy of the Maine Historic Preservation Commission, p. 126; (Nov. 1896), courtesy of the Maine Historic Preservation Commission, p. 103 top left, top right, and bottom

Sheldon, G. W., *Artistic Country Seats* (New York : D. Appleton, 1883–84), courtesy of the Athenaeum of Philadelphia, p. 28 top

Shettleworth, Jr., Earle G., p. vi top and bottom

Society for the Preservation of New England Antiquities: pp. 31, 137 top left and right, 138 top and bottom; photograph by Henry P. Benson (Hallidays Historic Photo Co.), 1916, p. 136 left; photograph by David Bohl, pp. 4, 140, 143, 144, 147; photograph by Elise Tyson Vaughan, 1903, pp. 142 left, 143 top, 145 top; photograph by Paul J. Weber, before 1929, pp. 142 right, 145 bottom

Stevens, John Calvin, and Albert Winslow Cobb, *Examples of American Domestic Architecture*, (New York, W. T. Comstock, 1889), courtesy of the Maine Historic Preservation Commission, p. 100

Stevens, Paul S.: ca. 1900, p. 112 bottom; ca. 1910, pp. 104, 105, 111 bottom, 112 top, 113 left and right; ca. 1930, p. 118

Thornton Academy Archives, p. 97 top and bottom

Weld, Mr. and Mrs. Stephen M., p. 14

York County Atlas (1872), courtesy of the Brick Store Museum, p. 11

Index